Etiquette PLUS

S0-BLQ-948

Polishing Life's Useful Skills

Inge P. Cannon

with Dr. Ronald Jay Cannon

Etiquette PLUS
Polishing Life's Useful Skills

©Copyright 1995 by Education PLUS+

All rights reserved. No part of this publication may be reproduced, stored in a retrieval system or transmitted in any form by any means, electronic, mechanical, photocopy, recording, or otherwise, without the prior written permission of Education PLUS+, except as provided by USA copyright law.

Scripture quotations noted NASB are taken from the *New American Standard Bible*, © 1960, 1962, 1963, 1968, 1971, 1972, 1973, 1975, 1977 by The Lockman Foundation. Used by permission. Scripture quotations noted KJV are taken from the *Authorized* (King James) *Version*.

Character definitions are adapted from *The American Heritage Dictionary of the English Language*, Third Edition,©1992 by Houghton Mifflin Company, and *American Dictionary of the English Languag*e, Facsimile Edition Noah Webster 1828, ©1967 by Rosalie J. Slater, published by Foundation for American Christian History.

Graphics by Aaron Fessler

Printed in the United States of America

ISBN 1-883669-26-X

$\mathscr{F}$oreword...

Etiquette—Is it "high privilege" or "panic"? Do you really need to teach these "stuffy rules" to your children? The dictionary defines privilege as "a right, favor, or immunity especially granted to an individual." Panic, in turn, is defined as "sudden, unreasonable, hysterical fear." Nothing in life can create privilege and eliminate panic more quickly than the comfortable practice of basic etiquette.

Learning the proprieties of life which can bring "a man before kings" is a vital part of character training for every adult and child. (See Proverbs 22:29 and Daniel 1:4.) This curriculum checklist examines "all the rules" in terms that are easy to remember and apply.

A unique feature of this etiquette guide is that the recommended procedures are tied to character qualities. The goal is to avoid learning rules for "rules' sake," but rather seeing each area of behavioral discipline as a function of Godly character.

There is much overlap in the definitions of character qualities, and we do not claim to be the only source for understanding the fine points where each is distinctive from another. However, we hope that grouping related qualities into clusters will assist you in teaching your children.

The verses provided for reference in understanding God's requirements for exercising each character quality are recommended for memorization in your child's curriculum.

Finally, you will note that the etiquette lessons are sorted by the age groups when most children should be able to begin mastering the required behavior. Obviously, most children will need ongoing reinforcement to adapt the particular rule through growing maturity levels. Characteristics of each age group are further explained in the *Growing in Wisdom & Stature* audiocassette series by Inge Cannon (available from *Education PLUS+*).

You may want to consider having a personal copy of the *Etiquette PLUS* checklist for each child. As he/she masters each procedure or area of understanding, check it off so that you can rejoice together in a job well done. When the list is completed, present the certificate of recognition along with the book to your young person as a memento and guide for reproducing these qualities in the lives of your grandchildren!

Etiquette PLUS
Polishing Life's Useful Skills

Seven character quality clusters provide the framework around which the rules of the etiquette curriculum checklist are organized:

Wisdom — Discernment, Discretion, Decisiveness

Attentiveness — Cautiousness, Alertness, Sensitivity, Resourcefulness

Obedience — Responsibility, Neatness, Consistency, Self-Control, Diligence, Punctuality, Thoroughness

Honesty — Truthfulness (Credibility), Innocence (Purity), Sincerity, Dependability, Integrity, Humility

Loyalty — Determination, Respect (Reverence), Fidelity (Faithfulness), Endurance

Gratefulness — Joyfulness, Cheerfulness, Service, Hospitality, Generosity, Enthusiasm, Contentment

Patience — Compassion, Longsuffering, Gentleness, Meekness, Deference, Kindness (Tolerance), Forgiveness, Flexibility, Availability

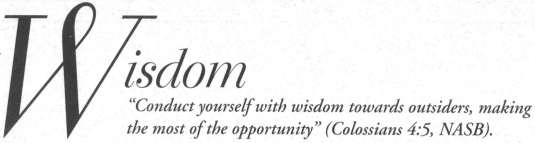

Wisdom

"Conduct yourself with wisdom towards outsiders, making the most of the opportunity" (Colossians 4:5, NASB).

Discernment

Discretion

Decisiveness

Wisdom

"Walk in wisdom toward them that are without, redeeming the time"
(Colossians 4:5, KJV).

The right use or exercise of knowledge; the choice of praiseworthy goals and the best means to accomplish them.

Wisdom is literally viewing the issues and questions of life from God's perspective. The textbook for learning God's point of view is the Bible.

"Happy is the man that findeth wisdom, and the man that getteth understanding"
(Proverbs 3:13, KJV).

Wisdom is the principal thing; therefore get wisdom: and with all thy getting get understanding" (Proverbs 4:7, KJV).

"For wisdom is better than jewels; and all desirable things cannot compare with her" (Proverbs 8:11, NASB).

"He who gets wisdom loves his own soul; he who keeps understanding will find good" (Proverbs 19:8, NASB).

"Wisdom strengthens a wise man more than ten rulers who are in a city" (Ecclesiastes 7:19, NASB).

"I, wisdom, dwell with prudence, and I find knowledge and discretion" (Proverbs 8:12, NASB).

"But if any of you lacks wisdom, let him ask of God, who gives to all men generously and without reproach, and it will be given to him" (James 1:5, NASB).

Discernment

"A wise man's heart discerneth both time and judgment" (Ecclesiastes 8:5b, KJV).

The ability to distinguish, discriminate, and make judgments: truth from falsehood, virtue from vice, sincerity from hypocrisy, positive impressions from negative ones, pure motives from impure ones, proper procedures from improper ones.

"Teach me good discernment and knowledge, for I believe in thy commandments" (Psalm 119:66, NASB).

"For if you cry for discernment, lift your voice for understanding; . . . then you will discern the fear of the Lord, and discover the knowledge of God. For the Lord gives wisdom . . ." (Proverbs 2:3-6, NASB).

Discretion

"My son, let not them depart from thine eyes: keep sound wisdom and discretion" (Proverbs 3:21, KJV).

Wise self-restraint in speech and behavior; free from ostentation or pretension; modest.

Discretion is a synonym for prudence: *"The prudent sees the evil and hides himself, but the naive go on, and are punished for it" (Proverbs 22:3, NASB).* Discretion enables a person to evaluate accurately what is correct and proper.

"A good man . . . will guide his affairs with discretion" (Psalm 112:5, KJV).

Decisiveness

"A double minded man is unstable in all his ways" (James 1:8, KJV).

The ability to reach definite conclusions and follow through with appropriate action. Decisiveness removes all doubt, resolves questions, and brings an end to controversy.

"I know your deeds, that you are neither cold nor hot; I would that you were cold or hot" (Revelation 3:15, NASB).

". . . How long will you hesitate between two opinions? If the Lord is God, follow Him . . ." (1 Kings 18:21, NASB)

"And if it is disagreeable in your sight to serve the Lord, choose for yourself today whom you will serve . . . but as for me and my house, we will serve the Lord" (Joshua 24:15, NASB).

Attentiveness

"However you want people to treat you, so treat them, for this is the Law and the Prophets" (Matthew 7:12, NASB).

Cautiousness

Alertness

Sensitivity

Resourcefulness

*A*ttentiveness

*"Make your ear attentive to wisdom, incline your heart to understanding"
(Proverbs 2:2, NASB).*

Intent hearing or close observation that results in a caring response; to listen or
see with understanding; literally, to pay attention.

The psalmist often prayed that God would be attentive to his petitions: *"Out of
the depths I have cried to Thee, O Lord. Lord, hear my voice! Let Thine ears be
attentive to the voice of my supplications" (Psalm 130:1-2, NASB).*

"If a brother or sister is without clothing and in need of daily food, and one of you says to them, 'Go in peace, be warmed and be filled,' and yet you do not give them what is necessary for their body, what use is that?" (James 2:15-16, NASB).

". . . Whatsoever ye would that men should do unto you, do ye even so to them: for this is the law and the prophets" (Matthew 7:12).

"Therefore everyone who hears these words of Mine, and acts upon them, may be compared to a wise man, who built his house upon the rock" (Matthew 7:24, NASB).

Cautiousness

"A wise man is cautious and turns away from evil, but a fool is arrogant and careless" (Proverbs 14:16, NASB).

Careful forethought to avoid danger or harm; vigilance to minimize risk.

A cautious person is heedful of circumstances and potential consequences: *"See then that ye walk circumspectly, not as fools, but as wise, Redeeming the time, because the days are evil"* (Ephesians 5:15-16, KJV).

"Beware lest any man spoil you through philosophy and vain deceit, after the tradition of men, after the rudiments of the world, and not after Christ. For in him dwelleth all the fullness of the Godhead bodily" (Colossians 2:8-9, KJV).

"Beware of the false prophets, who come to you in sheep's clothing, but inwardly are ravenous wolves" (Matthew 7:15, NASB).

"And in His teaching, He was saying: 'Beware of the scribes who like to walk around in long robes, and like respectful greetings in the market places, and chief seats in the synagogues, and places of honor at banquets, who devour widows' houses, and for appearance's sake offer long prayers; these will receive greater condemnation'" (Mark 12:38-40, NASB).

"And He said to them, 'Beware, and be on your guard against every form of greed; for not even when one has an abundance does his life consist of his possessions'" (Luke 12:15, NASB).

"You therefore, beloved, knowing this beforehand, be on your guard lest, being carried away by the error of unprincipled men, you fall from your own steadfastness, but grow in the grace and knowledge of our Lord and Savior Jesus Christ. To Him be the glory, both now and to the day of eternity. Amen." (2 Peter 3:17-18, NASB).

$\mathcal{A}$lertness

"Be on the alert, stand firm in the faith, act like men, be strong"
(1 Corinthians 16:13, NASB).

Watchful; vigilantly attentive; mentally responsive and perceptive; quick.

Alertness stresses speed in recognition and response. In Scripture, alertness is often associated with the need for prayer: *"Take ye heed, watch and pray: for ye know not when the time is" (Mark 13:33, KJV).*

"Watch ye therefore, and pray always. . ." (Luke 21:36, KJV).

"With all prayer and petition pray at all times in the Spirit, and with this in view, be on the alert with all perseverance and petition for all the saints" (Ephesians 6:18, NASB).

13

Sensitivity

"Let love be without hypocrisy. Abhor what is evil; cling to what is good. Be devoted to one another in brotherly love; give preference to one another in honor; not lagging behind in diligence, fervent in spirit, serving the Lord; rejoicing in hope; persevering in tribulation, devoted to prayer, contributing to the needs of the saints, practicing hospitality" (Romans 12:9-13, NASB).

Ability to appreciate or understand the circumstances, attitudes, or feelings of another and respond with sympathetic support. Sensitivity usually involves impressions or information received through the senses: hearing, seeing, touching, tasting, smelling.

When a person is called "sensitive" in a negative connotation, the word refers to being "touchy" or quick to take offense.

Resourcefulness

"And my God shall supply all your needs according to His riches in glory in Christ Jesus" (Philippians 4:19, NASB).

The ability to act effectively or imaginatively, especially in difficult situations.

Resourcefulness involves avoiding waste and putting to good use all available materials. Consider Jesus' feeding of five thousand men in addition to women and children with a lad's simple lunch. When the miracle was complete, Jesus instructed the disciples to gather the *"leftover fragments that nothing may be lost" (see John 6:1-13, NASB)*.

"And God is able to make all grace abound to you, that always having all sufficiency in everything, you may have an abundance for every good deed" (2 Corinthians 9:8, NASB).

Obedience

"Even a child is known by his doings, whether his work be pure, and whether it be right" (Proverbs 20:11, KJV).

Responsibility

Diligence

Neatness

Punctuality

Consistency

Thoroughness

Self-Control

O*bedience*

"Even a child is known by his doings, whether his work be pure, and whether it be right" (Proverbs 20:11, KJV).

Acceptance of and submission to authority; performing what is required and abstaining from what is prohibited.

An obedient person is one who yields to authority meekly without protest: *"Obey your leaders, and submit to them; for they keep watch over your souls, as those who will give an account. Let them do this with joy and not with grief, for this would be unprofitable for you" (Hebrews 13:17, NASB).*

"And Samuel said, 'Has the Lord as much delight in burnt offerings and sacrifices as in obeying the voice of the Lord? Behold, to obey is better than sacrifice, and to heed than the fat of rams. For rebellion is as the sin of divination, and insubordination is as iniquity and idolatry'"(1 Samuel 15:22-23a, NASB).

"My son, observe the commandment of your father, and do not forsake the teaching of your mother" (Proverbs 6:20, NASB).

"Servants, be obedient to them that are your masters according to the flesh, with fear and trembling, in singleness of your heart, as unto Christ; not with eyeservice, as menpleasers; but as the servants of Christ, doing the will of God from the heart; with good will doing service, as to the Lord, and not to men" (Ephesians 6:5-7, KJV).

"Let every person be in subjection to the governing authorities. For there is no authority except from God, and those which exist are established by God. Therefore he who resists authority has opposed the ordinance of God; and they who have opposed will receive condemnation upon themselves . . ." (Romans 13:1-10, NASB).

Responsibility

"For we are his workmanship, created in Christ Jesus unto good works, which God hath before ordained that we should walk in them" (Ephesians 2:10, KJV).

Duty; obligation; personal accountability; answerable.

A "responsible" person is one who performs duties in a satisfactory manner, adequately discharges obligations, or handles possessions in a trustworthy way.

". . . Each man's work will become evident; for the day will show it, because it is to be revealed by fire; and the fire itself will test the quality of each man's work. If any man's work which he has built upon it remains, he shall receive a reward. If any man's work is burned up, he shall suffer loss; but he himself shall be saved, yet so as through fire. Do you not know that you are a temple of God, and that the Spirit of God dwells in you?" (1 Corinthians 3:10-16, NASB).

Neatness

"But let all things be done properly and in an orderly manner"
(1 Corinthians 14:40, NASB).

Tidy; orderly and precise in procedure; systematic.

God provides in Scripture several illustrations of tasks completed in an orderly and systematic way: Creation, the building of the Ark, the construction of the Tabernacle, Israel's participation in sacrifices and feasts, Nehemiah's rebuilding Jerusalem's walls, and many more. Precise measurements, specifications for materials, and step-by-step instructions for procedures—all indicate how important orderliness is to God.

Consistency

"But be ye doers of the word, and not hearers only, deceiving your own selves"
(James 1:22, KJV).

The condition of being in agreement with itself; having logical coherence among the parts; reliability; steadiness; uniformity in results.

Consistency demands agreement between actions and words.   Once an instruction or obligation is understood, the responsibility to follow through rests upon every child of God: *"What use is it, my brethren, if a man says he has faith, but he has no works? Can that faith save him? . . . Even so faith, if it has no works, is dead, being by itself"* *(James 2:14-17, NASB).*

God is the ultimate example of consistency: *"Every good gift and every perfect gift is from above, and cometh down from the Father of lights, with whom is no variableness, neither shadow of turning" (James 1:17, KJV).*

"Jesus Christ is the same yesterday and today, yes and forever" (Hebrews 13:8, NASB).

Self-Control

"...Do you not know that your body is a temple of the Holy Spirit who is in you, whom you have from God, and that you are not your own? For you have been bought with a price: therefore glorify God in your body" (1 Corinthians 6:19-20, NASB).

To hold one's emotions, desires, or actions in restraint by an act of the will.

"Therefore do not let sin reign in your mortal body that you should obey its lusts, and do not go on presenting the members of your body to sin as instruments of unrighteousness; but present yourself to God as those alive from the dead, and your members as instruments of righteousness to God. For sin shall not be master over you, for you are not under law, but under grace" (Romans 6:12-14, NASB).

Paul described his goal to achieve self-control in terms of an athletic contest: *"Do you not know that those who run in a race all run, but only one receives the prize? Run in such a way that you may win. And everyone who competes in the games exercises self-control in all things. They then do it to receive a perishable wreath, but we our imperishable. Therefore I run in such a way, as not without aim; I box in such a way, as not beating the air; but I buffet my body and make it my slave, lest possibly, after I have preached to others, I myself should be disqualified"* (1 Corinthians 9:24-27, NASB).

"Let us behave properly as in the day, not in carousing and drunkenness, not in sexual promiscuity and sensuality, not in strife and jealousy. But put on the Lord Jesus Christ, and make no provision for the flesh in regard to its lusts" (Romans 13:13-14, NASB).

"I beseech you therefore, brethren, by the mercies of God, that ye present your bodies a living sacrifice, holy, acceptable unto God, which is your reasonable service. And be not conformed to this world: but be ye transformed by the renewing of your mind, that ye may prove what is that good, and acceptable, and perfect, will of God" (Romans 12:1-2, KJV).

"According to my earnest expectation and hope, that I shall not be put to shame in anything, but that with all boldness, Christ shall even now, as always, be exalted in my body, whether by life or by death" (Philippians 1:20, NASB).

"Thy word I have treasured in my heart, that I may not sin against Thee" (Psalm 119:11, NASB).

Diligence

"The hand of the diligent will rule, but the slack hand will be put to forced labor" *(Proverbs 12:24, NASB).*

Constant, painstaking effort applied to the pursuit of a specific goal; consistent application of energy.

The Christian life demands diligence in many areas to ensure productivity in personal growth, ministry, and business: *"And beside this, giving all diligence, add to your faith virtue, and to virtue knowledge . . ." (2 Peter 1:5-8, KJV).*

"Be diligent to present yourself approved to God as a workman who does not need to be ashamed, handling accurately the word of truth" (2 Timothy 2:15, NASB).

"Watch over your heart with all diligence, for from it flow the springs of life" (Proverbs 4:23, NASB).

"Therefore, brethren, be all the more diligent to make certain about His calling and choosing you; for as long as you practice these things, you will never stumble" (2 Peter 1:10, NASB).

"Thou hast ordained Thy precepts, that we should keep them diligently" (Psalm 119:4, NASB).

"He who diligently seeks good seeks favor, but he who searches after evil, it will come to him" (Proverbs 11:27, NASB).

"Seest thou a man diligent in his business? he shall stand before kings; he shall not stand before mean men" (Proverbs 22:29, KJV).

"Poor is he who works with a negligent hand, but the hand of the diligent makes rich" (Proverbs 10:4, NASB).

Without diligence it is impossible for ladies to demonstrate the charactertistics of the virtuous woman described in Proverbs 31:10-31.

God also instructs parents to practice diligence in training their sons and daughters: *"He who spares his rod hates his son, but he who loves him disciplines him diligently"* (Proverbs 13:24, NASB).

$\mathcal{P}$unctuality

*"To every thing there is a season, and a time to every purpose under the heaven"
(Ecclesiastes 3:1, KJV).*

Exactly at the time appointed; prompt, particularly with regard to time or promises.

Time is a function of life on earth. All natural processes have a designed timetable in which they are fulfilled. Delay or procrastination marks the person who is not diligent and therefore disobedient.

With regard to spiritual life, Scripture warns all men to make prompt decisions:
*". . .Behold, now is the accepted time; behold, now is the day of salvation"
(2 Corinthians 6:2, KJV).*

Thoroughness

"For which one of you, when he wants to build a tower, does not first sit down and calculate the cost, to see if he has enough to complete it? Otherwise, when he has laid a foundation and is not able to finish, all who observe it begin to ridicule him, saying, 'This man began to build and was not able to finish'"
(Luke 14:28-30, NASB).

Completing a task fully; painstakingly accurate; exhaustive (complete); absolute.

God's work is always thorough. He rested after completing His Creation and pronounced it "good." God's dealings with men are thorough as well. Therefore, David was able to pray, *"Wash me thoroughly from my iniquity, and cleanse me from my sin" (Psalm 51:2, NASB).*

The Apostle Paul also rejoiced with the Philippian Christians that God's work in perfecting His children for Heaven was thorough: *"Being confident of this very thing, that he which hath begun a good work in you will perform it until the day of Jesus Christ"* (Philippians 1:6, KJV).

God has given us in His Word all the resources we need to fulfill His will for our lives: *"All scripture is given by inspiration of God, and is profitable for doctrine, for reproof, for correction, for instruction in righteousness: that the man of God may be perfect, thoroughly furnished unto all good works"* (2 Timothy 3:16-17 KJV).

Jesus' ministry on earth provides a clear example of thoroughness. He often reminded the disciples that His mission was to complete the work the Father had sent Him to do: *"My meat is to do the will of him that sent me and to finish his work"* (John 4:34b, KJV). His prayer in the Garden of Gethsemane gave a similar testimony: *"I have glorified thee on earth: I have finished the work which thou gavest me to do"* (John 17:4, KJV).

On the cross He was able to state with complete certainty that He had finished all that God had sent Him to accomplish. Thus, we are able to recognize Him as *"the author and finisher of our faith"* (Hebrews 12:2, KJV).

Honesty

"Provide things honest in the sight of all men"
(Romans 12:17, KJV).

Truthfulness (Credibility)

Innocence (Purity)

Sincerity   Integrity

Dependability   Humility

*H*onesty

". . . Provide things honest in the sight of all men" (Romans 12:17, KJV).

Truthfulness, fairness in dealing with others, and refusal to engage in fraud or deceit (whether by statement or impression).

Honesty generally denotes the quality of being upright in principle and action. The term is usually applied to interaction with people or mutual dealing in the exchange of property.

"Finally, brethren, whatsoever things are true, whatsoever things are honest, whatsoever things are just, whatsoever things are pure, whatsoever things are lovely, whatsoever things are of good report; if there be any virtue, and if there be any praise, think on these things" (Philippians 4:8, KJV).

". . . *Study to be quiet, and to do your own business, and to work with your own hands, as we commanded you; that ye may walk honestly toward them that are without, and that ye may have lack of nothing*" *(1 Thessalonians 4:11-12, KJV).*

God instructs us to be diligent in praying for our leaders: *"For kings, and for all that are in authority; that we may lead a quiet and peaceable life in all godliness and honesty"* *(1 Timothy 2:2, KJV).*

Truthfulness (Credibility)

"Truthful lips will be established forever, but a lying tongue is only for a moment" (Proverbs 12:19, NASB).

Consistently reporting what conforms to fact or reality; reasoning according to accurate premises.

Truth is a comprehensive term that implies accuracy and honesty, a correct opinion, fidelity, constancy, virtue, exactness, and sincerity. Jesus said, *"I am the way, the truth, and the life"* (John 14:6a, KJV).

Credibility is that quality which renders it possible to be believed (involving no contradiction or obscurity).

"Lord, who shall abide in thy tabernacle? Who shall dwell in thy holy hill? He that walketh uprightly, and worketh righteousness, and speaketh the truth in his heart" (Psalm 15:1-2, KJV).

"A truthful witness saves lives, but he who speaks lies is treacherous" (Proverbs 14:25, NASB).

"For out of the abundance of the heart the mouth speaketh. . . But I say unto you, That every idle word that men shall speak, they shall give account thereof in the day of judgment. For by thy words thou shalt be justified, and by thy words thou shalt be condemned" (Matthew 12:34b, 36-37, KJV).

"Do not lie to one another, since you laid aside the old self with its evil practices" (Colossians 3:9, NASB).

Innocence (Purity)

"Blessed are the pure in heart, for they shall see God" (Matthew 5:8, KJV).

Not tainted with sin, naive, simple, lack of worldliness, without guile, clean.

Innocence denotes freedom from guilt or harm. Purity requires the absence of any extraneous elements; thus, the concept denotes "wholeness," and in a moral sense the word is used for chastity. Paul instructed Timothy to treat *the older women as mothers, and the younger women as sisters, in all purity" (1 Timothy 5:2, NASB).*

"Love not the world, neither the things that are in the world. If any man love the world, the love of the Father is not in him. For all that is in the world, the lust of the flesh, and the lust of the eyes, and the pride of life, is not of the Father, but is of the world" (1 John 2:15-16, KJV).

"To the pure, all things are pure; but to those who are defiled and unbelieving, nothing is pure, but both their mind and their conscience are defiled" (Titus 1:15, NASB).

"He who loves purity of heart and whose speech is gracious, the king is his friend" (Proverbs 22:11, NASB).

"But the goal of our instruction is love from pure heart and a good conscience and a sincere faith" (1 Timothy 1:5, NASB).

"Now flee from youthful lusts, and pursue righteousness, faith, love and peace, with those who call on the Lord with a pure heart" (2 Timothy 2:22, NASB).

"In all things show yourself to be an example of good deeds, with purity in doctrine, dignified, sound in speech which is beyond reproach, in order that the opponent may be put to shame, having nothing bad to say about us" (Titus 2:7-8, NASB).

"And everyone who has this hope fixed on Him purifies himself, just as He is pure" (1 John 3:3, NASB).

"Draw near to God and He will draw near to you. Cleanse your hands, you sinners; and purify your hearts, you double-minded" (James 4:8, NASB).

"How can a young man keep his way pure? By keeping it according to Thy word" (Psalm 119:9, NASB).

Sincerity

"Let us draw near with a sincere heart in full assurance of faith, having our hearts sprinkled clean from an evil conscience and our bodies washed with pure water" *(Hebrews 10:22, NASB).*

Honesty of mind or intention (motive); freedom from hypocrisy or false pretense; genuine, wholehearted, heartfelt.,

David recognized the importance of an undivided heart if he was to be sincere in glorifying God: *"Teach me thy way, O Lord; I will walk in thy truth: unite my heart to fear thy name. I will praise thee, O Lord my God, with all my heart: and I will glorify thy name for evermore" (Psalm 86:11-12, KJV)."*

Paul prayed for the Philippian Christians that their *"love may abound still more and more in real knowledge and all discernment, so that ye may approve the things that are excellent, in order to be sincere and blameless until the day of Christ"* (Philippians 1:9-10, NASB).

"Since you have in obedience to the truth purified your souls for a sincere love of the brethren, fervently love one another from the heart" (1 Peter 1:22, NASB).

"An hypocrite with his mouth destroyeth his neighbor" (Proverbs 11:9a, KJV).

"For what is the hope of the hypocrite, though he hath gained, when God taketh away his soul?" (Job 27:8, KJV).

"You hypocrite, first take the log out of your own eye, and then you will see clearly to take the speck out of your brother's eye" (Matthew 7:5, NASB).

"Therefore, putting aside all malice and all guile and hypocrisy and envy and all slander, like newborn babes, long for the pure milk of the word, that by it you may grow in respect to salvation, if you have tasted the kindness of the Lord" (1 Peter 2:1-3, NASB).

Dependability

"Lord, who shall abide in thy tabernacle? . . . He that sweareth to his own hurt, and changeth not" (Psalm 15:1a, 4b, KJV).

Trustworthy; reliable; inspiring full confidence.

Dependability is a reputation built over time as others observe how you function in the daily responsibilities of life. They will count on you in direct proportion to how you have fulfilled your word in past experiences.

"When you make a vow to God, do not be late in paying it, for He takes no delight in fools. Pay what you vow! It is better that you should not vow than that you should vow and not pay" (Ecclesiastes 5:4-5, NASB).

Integrity

"He who walks in integrity walks securely, but he who perverts his ways will be found out" (Proverbs 10:9, NASB).

Steadfast adherence to a strict moral or ethical code; absence of flaws in reasoning or process; soundness.

"Let integrity and uprightness preserve me; for I wait on thee" (Psalm 25:21, KJV).

"Vindicate me, O Lord, for I have walked in my integrity; and I have trusted in the Lord without wavering. Examine me, O Lord, and try me; test my mind and my heart" (Psalm 26:1-2, NASB).

". . . I will walk within my house in the integrity of my heart. I will set no worthless thing before my eyes" (Psalm 101:2-3a, NASB).

"The integrity of the upright will guide them, but the falseness of the treacherous will destroy them" (Proverbs 11:3, NASB).

"Many a man proclaims his own loyalty, but who can find a trustworthy man? A righteous man who walks in his integrity—how blessed are his sons after him" (Proverbs 20:6-7, NASB).

"The good man out of the good treasure of his heart brings forth what is good; and the evil man out of the evil treasure brings forth what is evil; for his mouth speaks from that which fills his heart" (Luke 6:45, NASB).

Humility

"Humble yourself in the presence of the Lord, and He will exalt you"
(James 4:10, NASB).

Marked by modesty in behavior, attitude, or spirit; not arrogant or prideful; accurate in recognizing the role of others in my success.

Humility demands complete honesty before God and transparency in our relationships with others. A humble person is able to admit his/her weaknesses and shortcomings and thus gain access to the resources available to fill in the gaps. A proud person has no access to God's grace, which is the unmerited favor of being equipped to desire and do God's will: *"For it is God which worketh in you both to will and to do of his good pleasure"* *(Philippians 2:13, KJV).*

"The reward of humility and the fear of the Lord are riches, honor, and life" (Proverbs 22:4, NASB).

". . . Clothe yourselves with humility toward one another, for God is opposed to the proud, but gives grace to the humble. Humble yourselves, therefore, under the mighty hand of God, that He may exalt you at the proper time" (1 Peter 5:5-6, NASB).

"The fear of the Lord is the instruction for wisdom, and before honor comes humility" (Proverbs 15:33, NASB).

"Pride goes before destruction, and a haughty spirit before stumbling. It is better to be of a humble spirit with the lowly, than to divide the spoil with the proud" (Proverbs 16:18-19, NASB).

"And whoever exalts himself shall be humbled; and whoever humbles himself shall be exalted" (Matthew 23:12, NASB).

Humility is required in any act of repentance toward God, whether individual or collective for an entire nation: *"If my people, which are called by my name, shall humble themselves, and pray, and seek my face, and turn from their wicked ways; then will I hear from heaven, and will forgive their sin, and will heal their land"* (2 Chronicles 7:14, KJV).

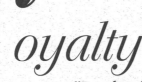

Loyalty

"Render therefore to all their dues: tribute to whom tribute is due; custom to whom custom; fear to whom fear; honour to whom honour" (Romans 13:7, KJV).

Determination

Respect (Reverence)

Fidelity (Faithfulness)

Endurance

Loyalty

"Render therefore to all their dues: tribute to whom tribute is due; custom to whom custom; fear to whom fear; honour to whom honour" *(Romans 13:7, KJV).*

Steadfast in allegiance; unshakable attachment to a person, cause or duty; devotion.

"For I delight in loyalty rather than sacrifice, and in the knowledge of God rather than burnt offerings" (Hosea 6:6, NASB).

". . . Every kingdom divided against itself is brought to desolation; and every city or house divided against itself shall not stand" (Matthew 12:25, KJV).

"Create in me a clean heart, O God, and renew a steadfast spirit within me" (Psalm 51:10, NASB).

Determination

"Therefore, my beloved brethren, be ye steadfast, unmoveable, always abounding in the work of the Lord, forasmuch as ye know that your labour is not in vain in the Lord" (1 Corinthians 15:58, KJV).

Firmness of purpose; resolute; having a fixed intention.

Determination sometimes refers to settling a question or influencing a conclusion. A jury does this when it determines a verdict. Jonathan Edwards used the word in this manner when he said, "The character of the soul is determined by the character of its God."

"But Daniel purposed in his heart that he would not defile himself . . ." (Daniel 1:8, KJV).

". . . I have purposed that my mouth will not transgress" (Psalm 17:3, NASB).

"My heart is fixed, O God, my heart is fixed . . ." (Psalm 57:7, KJV).

"He shall not be afraid of evil tidings: his heart is fixed, trusting in the Lord" (Psalm 112:7, KJV).

Respect (Reverence)

"Let nothing be done through strife or vainglory; but in lowliness of mind let each esteem other better than themselves" (Philippians 2:3, KJV).

Holding in high esteem, considered to be of real worth; responding with favor.

Reverence involves fear mingled with respect and esteem.

"Therefore, since we receive a kingdom which cannot be shaken, let us show gratitude, by which we may offer to God an acceptable service with reverence and awe" (Hebrews 12:28, NASB).

"I will meditate in thy precepts, and have respect unto thy ways" (Psalm 119:15, KJV).

"Hold thou me up, and I shall be safe: and I will have respect unto thy statutes continually (Psalm 119:117, KJV).

"But we request of you, brethren, that you appreciate those who diligently labor among you, and have charge over you in the Lord and give you instruction, and that you esteem them very highly in love because of their work. Live in peace with one another" (1 Thessalonians 5:12-13, NASB).

"Let as many servants as are under the yoke count their own masters worthy of all honour, that the name of God and his doctrine be not blasphemed" (1 Timothy 6:1, KJV).

"Nevertheless let every one of you in particular so love his wife even as himself; and the wife see that she reverence her husband" (Ephesians 5:33, KJV).

It is possible to show "respect" for the wrong things. Scripture teaches that *"there is no respect of persons with God"* (Romans 2:11, KJV) and warns us to avoid acting in a prejudicial manner or treating people with partiality: *"These things also belong to the wise. It is not good to have respect of persons in judgment"* (Proverbs 24:23, KJV). *"To show partiality is not good, because for a piece of bread a man will transgress"* (Proverbs 28:21, NASB).

"My brethren, do not hold your faith in our glorious Lord Jesus Christ with an attitude of personal favoritism. But if you show partiality, you are committing sin and are convicted by the law as transgressors" (James 2:1, 9, NASB).

Since man's values differ markedly from God's *". . . that which is highly esteemed among men is detestable in the sight of God"* (Luke 16:15b, NASB).

Fidelity (Faithfulness)

"Moreover it is required in stewards, that a man be found faithful" (1 Corinthians 4:2, KJV).

Constant in performance of obligations, duties or promises; true to one's word, conforming to both letter and spirit; not fickle.

A distinctive attribute of God's character is His faithfulness. Jeremiah wrote of this: *"It is of the Lord's mercies that we are not consumed, because his compassions fail not. They are new every morning: great is thy faithfulness"* (Lamentations 3:22-23, KJV).

"A faithful man will abound with blessings, but he who makes haste to be rich will not go unpunished" (Proverbs 28:20, NASB).

"He who is faithful in a very little thing is faithful also in much; and he who is unrighteous in a very little is unrighteous also in much" (Luke 16:10, NASB).

"And from everyone who has been given much shall much be required; and to whom they entrusted much, of him they will ask all the more" (Luke 12:48b, NASB).

". . . The Lord preserves the faithful . . ." (Psalm 31:23, NASB).

"Be thou faithful unto death, and I will give thee a crown of life" (Revelation 2:10b, KJV).

"And he who does not take his cross and follow after Me is not worthy of Me" (Matthew 10:38, NASB).

The Apostle Paul looked forward to the rewards of faithfulness when he would stand before the Lord: *"I have fought the good fight, I have finished the course, I have kept the faith; in the future there is laid up for me a crown of righteousness, which the Lord, the righteous Judge, will award to me on that day; and not only to me, but also to all who have loved His appearing"* (2 Timothy 4:7-8, NASB).

Endurance

"Thou therefore endure hardness, as a good soldier of Jesus Christ"
(2 Timothy 2:3, KJV).

Withstanding hardship; carrying on despite difficulty, suffering patiently without yielding; persevering.

"But you, be sober in all things, endure hardship, do the work of an evangelist, fulfill your ministry"
(2 Timothy 4:5, NASB).

"Blessed is the man that endureth temptation: for when he is tried, he shall receive the crown of life, which the Lord hath promised to them that love him" (James 1:12, KJV).

"But he that shall endure unto the end, the same shall be saved" (Matthew 24:13, KJV).

"For this is thankworthy, if a man for conscience toward God endure grief, suffering wrongfully" (1 Peter 2:19, KJV).

"It is for discipline that you endure; God deals with you as with sons; for what son is there whom his father does not discipline?" (Hebrews 12:7, NASB).

"[Love] bears all things, believes all things, hopes all things, endures all things. Love never fails" (1 Corinthians 13:7-8a, NASB).

Gratefulness

"In every thing give thanks: for this is the will of God in Christ Jesus concerning you" (1 Thessalonians 5:18, KJV).

Joyfulness

Cheerfulness

Service

Hospitality

Generosity

Enthusiasm

Contentment

Gratefulness

"In everything give thanks: for this is the will of God in Christ Jesus concerning you" (1 Thessalonians 5:18, KJV).

Thankful; expressing gratitude; willing to acknowledge and repay benefits.

"And let the peace of Christ rule in your hearts, to which indeed you were called in one body; and be thankful" (Colossians 3:15, NASB).

"Giving thanks always for all things unto God and the Father in the name of our Lord Jesus Christ" (Ephesians 5:20, KJV).

"Be careful for nothing; but in every thing by prayer and supplication with thanksgiving let your requests be made known unto God" (Philippians 4:6, KJV).

Joyfulness

"A joyful heart is good medicine, but a broken spirit dries up the bones"
(Proverbs 17:22, NASB).

A sense of gladness, often brought about by success, blessing, gratification of desire, or mission accomplished; exultation, exhilaration of spirit; a glorious and triumphant state.

"Restore unto me the joy of thy salvation; and uphold me with thy free spirit" (Psalm 51:12, KJV).

"I will greatly rejoice in the Lord, my soul shall be joyful in my God; for he that clothed me with the garments of salvation, he hath covered me with the robes of righteousness, as a bridegroom decketh himself with ornaments, and as a bride adorneth herself with her jewels" (Isaiah 61:10, KJV).

"Looking unto Jesus the author and finisher of our faith; who for the joy that was set before him endured the cross, despising the shame, and is set down at the right hand of the throne of God" (Hebrews 12:2, KJV).

"The Lord is my strength and my shield; my heart trusteth in him and I am helped: therefore my heart greatly rejoiceth; and with my song will I praise him" (Psalm 28:7, KJV).

"Weeping may endure for a night, but joy cometh in the morning" (Psalm 30:5b, KJV).

"They that sow in tears shall reap in joy" (Psalm 126:5, KJV).

"These things have I spoken unto you, that my joy might remain in you, and that your joy might be full" (John 15:11, KJV).

"The father of the righteous shall greatly rejoice: and he that begetteth a wise child shall have joy of him" (Proverbs 23:24, KJV).

Cheerfulness

"A merry heart maketh a cheerful countenance: but by sorrow of the heart the spirit is broken" **(Proverbs 15:13, KJV).**

An attitude dispelling gloom, sorrow, or silence; animated with a sense of happiness; pleasant; in good humor.

"These things I have spoken unto you, that in me ye might have peace. In the world ye shall have tribulation: but be of good cheer; I have overcome the world" (John 16:33, KJV).

"Let each one do just as he has purposed in his heart; not grudgingly or under compulsion; for God loves a cheerful giver" (2 Corinthians 9:7, NASB).

"Having then gifts differing according to the grace that is given to us . . . he that showeth mercy, with cheerfulness" (Romans 12:6-8, KJV).

Service

". . . Whoever wishes to become great among you shall be your servant; and whoever wishes to be first among you shall be slave of all. For even the Son of Man did not come to be served but to serve, and to give His life a ransom for many" (Mark 10:42-45, NASB).

To meet the needs of others; to be employed in a specific purpose; to supply what is required; to fulfill a duty.

Service often involves the labor of body and/or mind in response to the command of a superior. In this sense there are two types of service: voluntary (that of hired servants or by contract) and involuntary (that of slaves who work by compulsion).

Because excellent service demands wholeheartedness, Jesus warned that *"No one can serve two masters; for either he will hate the one and love the other, or he will hold to one and despise the other. You cannot serve God and mammon" (Matthew 6:24, NASB).*

"Truly, truly, I say to you, unless a grain of wheat falls into the earth and dies, it remains by itself alone; but if it dies, it bears much fruit. He who loves his life loses it; and he who hates his life in this world shall keep it to life eternal. If anyone serves Me, let him follow Me; and where I am, there shall My servant also be; if anyone serves Me, the Father will honor him" (John 12:24-26, NASB).

"For you were called to freedom, brethren; only do not turn your freedom into an opportunity for the flesh, but through love serve one another" (Galatians 5:13, NASB).

Hospitality

"Be hospitable to one another without complaint" (I Peter 4:9, NASB).

Cordial and generous treatment of guests with no desire of reward or return favor.

Jesus taught his disciples that meeting the needs of others would be considered by the Father as having ministered to the Lord Himself: *"Then the righteous will answer Him, saying, 'Lord, when did we see You hungry, and feed You, or thirsty, and give You drink? And when did we see You a stranger, and invite You in, or naked, and clothe You? And when did we see You sick, or in prison, and come to You?' And the King will answer and say to them, 'Truly I say to you, to the extent that you did it to one of these brothers of Mine, even the least of them, you did it to Me'" (Matthew 25:37-40, NASB).*

Paul instructed both Timothy and Titus that hospitality was a requirement for leadership in the church: *"An overseer, then, must be above reproach, the husband of one wife, temperate, prudent, respectable, hospitable, able to teach"* (1 Timothy 3:2, NASB).

"For the overseer must be above reproach as God's steward, not self-willed, not quick-tempered, not addicted to wine, not pugnacious, not fond of sordid gain, but hospitable, loving what is good, sensible, just, devout, self-controlled, holding fast the faithful word which is in accordance with the teaching, that he may be able both to exhort in sound doctrine and to refute those who contradict" (Titus 1:7-9, NASB).

Special blessings are reserved for those who are generous in caring for strangers: *"Do not neglect to show hospitality to strangers, for by this some have entertained angels without knowing it"* (Hebrews 13:2, NASB).

Generosity

". . . Freely you received, freely give" (Matthew 10:8b, NASB).

Marked by abundance in giving; bountiful; overflowing.

Generosity is the means by which God's children "lay up treasure in heaven" rather than striving to accumulate wealth on earth. As we invest our resources in the lives of others around us, God counts our generosity in terms of heavenly rewards, and we realign our values: *"For where your treasure is, there will your heart be also" (see Matthew 6:19-21, NASB).*

"Now this I say, he who sows sparingly shall also reap sparingly; and he who sows bountifully shall also reap bountifully. Let each one do just as he has purposed in his heart, not grudgingly or under compulsion, for God loves a cheerful giver" (2 Corinthians 9:6-7, NASB).

In warning His disciples of the dangers of materialism, Jesus explained that it is hard for those who focus their lives on gaining wealth to enter heaven. When the rich, young ruler came to Jesus, seeking eternal life, the Master instructed him, *"One thing you still lack; sell all that you possess, and distribute it to the poor, and you shall have treasure in heaven; and come, follow Me" (see Luke 18:18-22, NASB).* While giving to others is not a means of earning salvation, a generous heart indicates willingness to trust God for the provision of resources and a right perspective for the use of wealth.

God's character is marked by generosity—even toward those who do not hold Him in high esteem. We are commanded to emulate our Heavenly Father: *"But I say to you, love your enemies, and pray for those who persecute you in order that you may be sons of your Father who is in heaven; for He causes His sun to rise on the evil and the good, and sends rain on the righteous and the unrighteous" (Matthew 5:44-45, NASB).*

"He who is generous will be blessed, for he gives some of his food to the poor" (Proverbs 22:9, NASB).

"The generous man will be prosperous, and he who waters will himself be watered" (Proverbs 11:25, NASB).

"Cast thy bread upon the waters: for thou shalt find it after many days" (Ecclesiastes 11:1, KJV).

"Give to him who asks of you, and do not turn away from him who wants to borrow from you" (Matthew 5:42, NASB).

Enthusiasm

"Whatsoever thy hand findeth to do, do it with thy might; for there is no work, nor device, nor knowledge, nor wisdom, in the grave, whither thou goest" *(Ecclesiastes 9:10, KJV).*

Great excitement or interest for a subject; passionate pursuit of a goal; wholehearted in productivity or giving of energy.

The example for our wholehearted, enthusiastic obedience in fulfilling God's will is the Lord Jesus Christ, *"Who gave Himself for us, that He might redeem us from every lawless deed and purify for Himself a people for His own possession, zealous for good deeds" (Titus 2:14, NASB).*

"I can do all things through Christ which strengtheneth me" (Philippians 4:13, KJV).

Contentment

"Let your character be free from the love of money, being content with what you have; for He Himself has said, 'I will never desert you, nor will I ever forsake you'" (Hebrews 13:5, NASB).

Desiring no more than one has; satisfied with things as they are; at rest; peaceful.

The Apostle Paul gave testimony to the importance of this lesson in a Christian's life: *"Not that I speak from want; for I have learned to be content in whatever circumstances I am" (Philippians 4:11, NASB).*

"But godliness with contentment is great gain. For we brought nothing in this world, and it is certain that we can carry nothing out. And having food and raiment let us be therewith content"
(1 Timothy 6:6-8, KJV).

". . . Beware, and be on your guard against every form of greed; for not even when one has an abundance does his life consist of his possessions" (Luke 12:15, NASB).

"The Lord is my shepherd; I shall not want . . ." (Psalm 23, KJV).

Patience

"And we urge you, brethren, admonish the unruly, encourage the fainthearted, help the weak, be patient with all men" (1 Thessalonians 5:14, NASB).

Compassion

Longsuffering

Gentleness

Meekness

Deference

Kindness

(Tolerance)

Forgiveness

Flexibility

Availability

*P*atience

"And we urge you, brethren, admonish the unruly, encourage the fainthearted, help the weak, be patient with all men" (1 Thessalonians 5:14, NASB).

Suffering affliction, pain, toil, calamity, or other evil with a calm, unruffled temper; enduring difficulty without complaint; waiting for justice or reward without setting deadlines for fulfillment.

"Love is patient, love is kind, and is not jealous; love does not brag and is not arrogant, does not act unbecomingly; it does not seek its own, is not provoked, does not take into account a wrong suffered, does not rejoice in unrighteousness, but rejoices with the truth, bears all things, believes all things, hopes all things, endures all things" (1 Corinthians 13:4-7, NASB).

"... We have not ceased to pray for you and to ask that you may be filled with the knowledge of His will in all spiritual wisdom and understanding, so that you may walk in a manner worthy of the Lord, to please Him in all respects, bearing fruit in every good work and increasing in the knowledge of God; strengthened with all power, according to His glorious might for the attaining of all steadfastness and patience ..." (Colossians 1:9-12, NASB).

"My brethren, count it all joy when you fall into divers temptations; knowing this, that the trying of your faith worketh patience. But let patience have her perfect work, that ye may be perfect and entire, wanting nothing" (James 1:2-4, KJV).

"You too be patient; strengthen your hearts, for the coming of the Lord is at hand. Do not complain, brethren, against one another, that you yourselves may not be judged; behold, the Judge is standing right at the door" (James 5:8-9, NASB).

"The Lord is not slow about His promise, as some count slowness, but is patient toward you, not wishing for any to perish but for all to come to repentance" (2 Peter 3:9, NASB).

Compassion

"And of some have compassion, making a difference" (Jude 22, KJV).

Having a heart that is tender and moved easily by the distresses, sufferings, needs, and infirmities of others; sympathy coupled with the desire to provide relief or resolution.

In Scripture, compassion is usually pity blended with forgiveness. God's covenant relationship with Israel demonstrates this: *"But He, being compassionate, forgave their iniquity, and did not destroy them"* (Psalm 78:38, NASB).

Jesus illustrated this same concept in the parable of the prodigal son: *"And he got up and came to his father. But while he was still a long way off, his father saw him, and felt compassion for him, and ran and embraced him, and kissed him"* (Luke 15:20, NASB).

"And so, as those who have been chosen of God, holy and beloved, put on a heart of compassion, kindness, humility, gentleness, and patience; bearing with one another, and forgiving each other, whoever has a complaint against anyone; just as the Lord forgave you, so also should you" (Colossians 3:12-13, NASB).

"Finally, be ye all of one mind, having compassion one of another, love as brethren, be pitiful, be courteous: not rendering evil for evil, or railing for railing: but contrariwise blessing; knowing that ye are thereunto called, that ye should inherit a blessing" (1 Peter 3:8-9, KJV).

"Rejoice with those who rejoice, and weep with those who weep" (Romans 12:15, NASB).

Longsuffering

"I . . . beseech you that ye walk worthy of the vocation wherewith ye are called, with all lowliness and meekness, with longsuffering, forbearing one another in love; endeavouring to keep the unity of the Spirit in the bond of peace" (Ephesians 4:1-3, KJV).

Bearing injuries or provocation for a long time; not easily provoked; merciful. David describes God's compassion and graciousness as longsuffering which is *"plenteous in mercy and truth" (Psalm 86:15, KJV).* We exhibit the quality of "longsuffering" when we show mercy toward others. *"Blessed are the merciful: for they shall obtain mercy" (Matthew 5:7, KJV).*

"He hath shown thee, O man, what is good; and what doth the Lord require of thee, but to do justly, and to love mercy, and to walk humbly with thy God?" (Micah 6:8, KJV).

Gentleness

"And the servant of the Lord must not strive; but be gentle unto all men, apt to teach, patient (2 Timothy 2:24, KJV).

Considerate of others with softness of manner, mildness of temper, and sweetness of disposition; not harsh or severe; soothing.

"A gentle answer turns away wrath, but a harsh word stirs up anger" (Proverbs 15:1, NASB).
"By forbearance a ruler may be persuaded, and a soft tongue breaks the bone" (Proverbs 25:15, NASB).
"A soothing tongue is a tree of life, but perversion in it crushes the spirit" (Proverbs 15:4, NASB).

"But the wisdom that is from above is first pure, then peaceable, gentle, and easy to be entreated, full of mercy and good fruits, without partiality, and without hypocrisy" (James 3:17, KJV).

"But the fruit of the Spirit is love, joy, peace, longsuffering, gentleness, goodness, faith, meekness, temperance: against such there is no law" (Galatians 5:22-23, KJV).

*M*eekness

"Blessed are the meek: for they shall inherit the earth" (Matthew 5:5, KJV).

Showing humility and a submissive attitude; literally, bringing strength under control or restraint.

Jesus invites all believers to *"Take my yoke upon you, and learn of me; for I am meek and lowly in heart: and ye shall find rest unto your souls. For my yoke is easy, and my burden is light"* (Matthew 11:29-30, KJV).

"Put them in mind to be subject to principalities and powers, to obey magistrates, to be ready to every good work, to speak evil of no man, to be no brawlers, but gentle, showing all meekness unto all men" (Titus 3:1-2. KJV)

"For the love of money is the root of all evil: . . . But thou, O man of God, flee these things; and follow after righteousness, godliness, faith, love, patience, meekness" (1 Timothy 6:10-11, KJV).

Women are especially encouraged to recognize the importance of inner beauty which cannot be taken away: *"But let it be the hidden man of the heart, and that which is not corruptible, even the ornament of a meek and quiet spirit, which is in the sight of God of great price"* (1 Peter 3:4, KJV).

$\mathcal{D}$eference

"And be subject to one another in the fear of Christ" (Ephesians 5:21, NASB).

Submissive or courteous yielding to the opinions of others; respect.

"Submit yourselves for the Lord's sake to every human institution, whether to the king as the one in authority, or to governors as sent by him for the punishment of evildoers and the praise of those who do right. For such is the will of God that by doing right you may silence the ignorance of foolish men. Act as free men, and do not use your freedom as a covering for evil, but use it as bondslaves of God. Honor all men; love the brotherhood, fear God, honor the king" (1 Peter 2:13-17, NASB).

"In the same way, you wives, be submissive to your own husbands so that even if any of them are disobedient to the word, they may be won without a word by the behavior of their wives"
(1 Peter 3:1, NASB).

"Now accept the one who is weak in faith, but not for the purpose of passing judgment on his opinions. . . . For not one of us lives for himself, and not one dies for himself; for if we live, we live for the Lord, or if we die, we die for the Lord; therefore whether we live or die, we are the Lord's. . . . But you, why do you judge your brother? Or you again, why do you regard your brother with contempt? For we shall all stand before the judgment seat of God. . . . Therefore let us not judge one another anymore, but rather determine this—not to put an obstacle or a stumbling block in a brother's way. I know and am convinced in the Lord Jesus that nothing is unclean in itself; but to him who thinks anything to be unclean, to him it is unclean. . . . So then let us pursue the things which make for peace and the building up of one another. . . ." (Romans 14:1-23, NASB).

Kindness (Tolerance)

"And be ye kind one to another, tenderhearted, forgiving one another, even as God for Christ's sake hath forgiven you" (Ephesians 4:32, KJV).

That disposition which delights in contributing to the happiness of others and is exercised cheerfully in granting their wishes, supplying their wants, or alleviating their distresses; warm-heartedness; consideration; agreeableness; benevolence.

"She opens her mouth in wisdom, and the teaching of kindness is on her tongue" (Proverbs 31:26, NASB).

"And the Lord's bond-servant must not be quarrelsome, but be kind to all, able to teach, patient when wronged, with gentleness correcting those who are in opposition, if perhaps God may grant them repentance leading to the knowledge of the truth, and they may come to their senses and escape from the snare of the devil, having been held captive by him to do his will" (2 Timothy 2:24-26, NASB).

Forgiveness

"And forgive us our debts, as we also have forgiven our debtors"
(Matthew 6:12, NASB).

The act of pardoning an offender, by which he is considered as not guilty; to absolve from payment or release from a debt, fine or penalty.

God deals mercifully with His children, thus continually demonstrating what true forgiveness really means: *"He has not dealt with us according to our sins, nor rewarded us according to our iniquities. For as high as the heavens are above the earth, so great is His lovingkindness toward those who fear Him. As far as the east is from the west, so far has He removed our transgressions from us. Just as a father has compassion on his children, so the Lord has compassion on those who fear Him. For He Himself knows our frame; He is mindful that we are but dust" (Psalm 103:10-14, NASB).*

The person who refuses to forgive another literally destroys the very bridge over which he must cross to experience God's mercy: *"If Thou, Lord, shouldst mark iniquities, O Lord, who could stand? But there is forgiveness with Thee, That Thou mayest be feared"* (Psalm 130:3-4, NASB).

"For if you forgive men for their transgressions, your heavenly Father will also forgive you. But if you do not forgive men, then your Father will not forgive your transgressions" (Matthew 6:14-15, NASB).

"Then Peter came and said to Him, 'Lord, how often shall my brother sin against me and I forgive him? Up to seven times?' Jesus said to him, 'I do not say to you, up to seven times, but up to seventy times seven. For this reason the kingdom of heaven may be compared to a certain king who wished to settle accounts with his slaves . . .'" (Matthew 18:21-35, NASB).

Flexibility

". . . I have become all things to all men, that I may by all means save some"
(1 Corinthians 9:20-22, NASB).

The quality of bending; being responsive to change; adaptable; elastic.

The key to flexibility is obeying God's direction in adapting to needs around you. While the testimony of Paul was that *"to the Jews I became as a Jew, that I might win Jews; to those who are under the Law, as under the Law, though not being myself under the Law, that I might win those who are under the Law" (1 Corinthians 9:20, NASB),* Peter struggled with the request to be flexible in ministering the gospel to Gentiles.

God answered his resistance with a special message. Three times Peter saw in a dream the semblance of a sheet with many "unclean" animals. God spoke to him: *"Arise, Peter, kill and eat!"* As a faithful Jew under the Law, Peter responded, *"By no means, Lord, for I have never eaten anything unholy and unclean."* As Peter reflected on the dream and God's words, Cornelius' messengers arrived. Peter then realized that he was called to share the Gospel with Cornelius. *(See Acts 10:1-23 and Acts 11:1-18.)*

*A*vailability

"Preach the word; be ready in season and out of season; reprove, rebuke, exhort, with great patience and instruction" (2 Timothy 4:2, NASB).

Ready for use; at hand; willing to serve.

"Then I heard the voice of the Lord, saying, 'Whom shall I send, and who will go for us?' Then I said, 'Here am I, send me!'" (Isaiah 6:8, NASB).

"And He was saying to them, 'The harvest is plentiful, but the laborers are few; therefore beseech the Lord of the harvest to send out laborers into His harvest'" (Luke 10:2, NASB).

"But sanctify Christ as Lord in your hearts, always being ready to make a defense to everyone who asks you to give an account for the hope that is in you, yet with gentleness and reverence" (1 Peter 3:15, NASB).

Etiquette PLUS
Polishing Life's Useful Skills

"Let no one look down on your youthfulness, but rather in speech, conduct, love, faith and purity, show yourself an example of those who believe" (1 Timothy 4:12, NASB).

"But wilt thou know, O vain man, that faith without works is dead?" (James 2:20, KJV).

"I have no greater joy than to hear that my children walk in truth" (3 John 4, KJV).

"You are our letter, written in our hearts, known and read by all men; being manifested that you are a letter of Christ, cared for by us, written not with ink, but with the spirit of the living God, not on tablets of stone, but on tablets of human hearts" (2 Corinthians 3:2-3, NASB).

We live in a day when much is being said about rules of any kind—should we have them? Who should determine them? What should they be? What about the liberty we have in Christ? What about testimony and reputation?

The person who wants fewer "regulations" accuses, "legalism"; the one who sees controls as being necessary says, "standards." Some call for "being natural" and accepting one another just as we are. Others value personal discipline and "proper" order in relationships. One can almost identify a person's perspective by his/her choice of terms.

While it is true that many of the details in etiquette procedures are somewhat arbitrary and can be adjusted as needs arise, the bottom line is that each "rule" reflects an attitude or character quality which reveals an individual's core values and personal beliefs. The following thoughts should help to set a foundation for determining which rules of etiquette or "social graces," as they are often called, will be important to your family.

First, consider the thought that "others may; you may not." It's a simple reality that God sometimes places limits on His servants that are set especially for the development of their lives as leaders. Leaders literally live in goldfish bowls—everyone sees how and where they swim!

Are you willing to set aside a personal habit or choice to help someone else grow in the Lord? Can you view this as a high calling from God, rather than a straight jacket? Will you view the practice of details that sometimes feel needlessly "picky" as a means of demonstrating the character of Christ in your life?

Second, there are many "levels" of rules in the world of etiquette and in every walk of life. Much irritation of spirit can come as a result of not understanding these. It will be helpful to your children if, as they grow older, you help them identify the category of each etiquette rule you are striving to learn and practice.

- *Convictional* or *moral* directives deal with issues that are plainly right or wrong according to the changeless Word of God. These may never be adjusted. Etiquette rules which fall into this category involve propriety between men and women, honesty in communication, integrity in ethics, and careful fulfillment of promises.

- *Efficiency* directives are outlined for the convenience of a group that is trying to "get the job" done smoothly. This group can be a family, work team, friendship, or any other unit of people. The larger the group or more involved the relationship, the greater will be the emphasis on procedural regulations. These rules may be adapted whenever necessary to enhance communication or improve efficiency. Etiquette rules in this category deal with being punctual, organized, neat, etc. at work, in travel, during leisure activities and with guests.

- *Deference* or *consideration* directives deal with how others feel when I behave toward them in a given manner. These etiquette rules enable a person to practice the "golden rule" in avoiding offense.

- *Reputational* concerns deal with the appearance of things and the associations which things have. These rules involve setting minimum standards so that individual and organizational images are controlled. As such, these are often the most difficult requirements of all, because people have so many opinions of what is best. Just remember that God's Word teaches us to "avoid every appearance of evil" and to be moderate or balanced in good things. Etiquette rules in this category involve honesty with money and things, chaperones to communicate propriety and protection, and dependability in fulfilling responsibilities.

Third, it would be ideal if everyone matured spiritually and emotionally at the same rate. It would also be ideal if an exhaustive list of "do's" and "don'ts" could be mastered. But life's situations often involve judgment calls that seem to fall between the cracks between ideals which are specified. Teach your children that it is a mark of maturity when they can evaluate the "gray areas" or questionable things by God's direction with questions like these: Will this habit/activity build my life? Will it bind me in any way? Is it the best for me? (Rather than asking "what's wrong with an action or activity," consider carefully "what's right about it?")

Finally, you have heard many times that "actions speak louder than words." But most people forget that there is something that speaks even louder than actions—that is, a person's spirit or attitude. Every rule of etiquette for Christians should be derived to communicate the core message of what we believe and the Lord Whom we serve.

For example, the practice of "chivalry" or gentlemanly conduct—whether given by a man or received graciously by a woman— is really a testimony to what we believe about the distinction between men and women. The fact that we "dress up" for a worship service, wedding, or funeral allows us to show respect to the one being honored in each context. Simple table manners give us the opportunity to present ourselves in the polished manner that we would like to observe in others, for no one enjoys witnessing crude behavior during a meal.

Each choice demonstrates more than just our ability to learn rules and adopt habits. The practices themselves clearly demonstrate our philosophy of life, for the true test of what a person believes lies in his/her actions rather than words. When the rules are mastered in terms of the core message demonstrated by the resulting actions, our children are then placed in the best position to make the cross-cultural adjustments which may be necessary at some future time.

Successful training always involves instruction, reinforcement, correction, and consistent example. There really are no shortcuts. Self-discipline is a lifelong exercise. In this we encourage you to treat your children as though you won't have them next year and train them as though they won't have you next year.

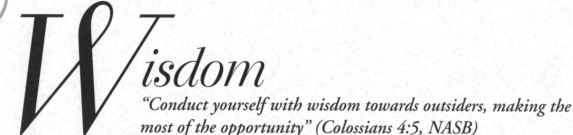

Wisdom

"Conduct yourself with wisdom towards outsiders, making the most of the opportunity" (Colossians 4:5, NASB)

Conception - Age 3

❏ Cry only for a real need.

". . . A time to keep silence, and a time to speak" (Ecclesiastes 3:7, KJV).

❏ Don't interrupt when others speak.

"Even a fool, when he keeps silent, is considered wise; when he closes his lips, he is counted prudent" (Proverbs 17:28, NASB).

❏ Play quietly.

"He that blesseth his friend with a loud voice . . . it shall be counted a curse to him" (Proverbs 27:14, KJV).

Attentiveness

"However you want people to treat you, so treat them, for this is the Law and the Prophets" (Matthew 7:12, NASB).

Conception - Age 3

❑   Respect the limits of the word "no."

❑   Listen with eye contact when someone speaks to you.

❑   Answer when someone speaks to you.

❑   Ask permission before touching or taking things.

❑   Keep yourself occupied happily in play.

Obedience

"Even a child is known by his doings, whether his work be pure, and whether it be right" (Proverbs 20:11, KJV).

Conception - Age 3

❑   Avoid temper tantrums.
"He that hath no rule over his own spirit is like a city that is broken down, and without walls" (Proverbs 25:28, KJV).

❑   Dress yourself neatly.

❑   Pick up toys. Put one away before taking another

     "But let all things be done properly and in an orderly manner" (1 Corinthians 14:40, NASB).

❑   Ask for things you want.

❏   Wash your face and hands before and after meals.

❏   Don't complain about food. Never refuse to eat food given to you.
[Note to parents: Allergies and personal beliefs should be explained graciously.]
"Do all things without murmurings and disputings" (Philippians 2:14, KJV).

"If one of the unbelievers invites you, and you wish to go, eat anything that is set before you, without asking questions for conscience' sake. . . . Whether, then, you eat or drink or whatever you do, do all to the glory of God (1 Corinthians 10:27, 31, NASB)

❏   Eat with a spoon or fork. Hold each utensil properly.

❏   Brush your teeth after each meal or snack.

❏   Learn how to use the toilet (when ready).

❏   Come immediately when called; go when sent.
"Children, obey your parents in the Lord: for this is right" (Ephesians 6:1, KJV).

*H*onesty

"Provide things honest in the sight of all men"
(Romans 12:17, KJV).

Conception - Age 3

☐   Respect your body as God's special gift to you that is not for others to see.
Tell your parents if anyone ever touches you in an improper way.

"I will praise thee; for I am fearfully and wonderfully made: marvellous are thy works; and that my soul knoweth right well" (Psalm 139:14, KJV).

Loyalty

"Render therefore to all their dues: tribute to whom tribute is due; custom to whom custom; fear to whom fear; honour to whom honour" (Romans 13:7, KJV).

Conception - Age 3

❑ Say hello with eye contact when meeting people. Say goodbye when leaving.

❑ Greet grandparents with a hug and kiss.

Gratefulness

"In every thing give thanks: for this is the will of God in Christ Jesus concerning you" (1 Thessalonians 5:18, KJV).

Conception - Age 3

❏ Say "please, thank you, I love you" at the right times.
"Let no unwholesome word proceed from your mouth, but only such a word as is good for edification according to the need of the moment, that it may give grace to those who hear" (Ephesians 4:29, NASB).

❏ Share toys with siblings and friends.

Patience

"And we urge you, brethren, admonish the unruly, encourage the fainthearted, help the weak, be patient with all men" (1 Thessalonians 5:14, NASB).

Conception - Age 3

❏ Use the words "I did wrong" to acknowledge misdeeds.
   ". . . I will be sorry for my sin" (Psalm 38:18, KJV).

❏ Use kind words toward siblings, pets, and friends.
   "Be ye kind one to another, tenderhearted . . ." (Ephesians 4:32, KJV).

❏ Wait quietly for your turn in games or when treats are distributed.

*W*isdom

"Conduct yourself with wisdom towards outsiders, making the most of the opportunity" (Colossians 4:5, NASB)

Ages 4-5

❑ Respect the Bible as God's Word. Handle it with care and with honor.
"*. . . My heart stands in awe of Thy words" (Psalm 119:161, NASB)*.

❑ Participate quietly in prayer time.
[Note to parents: Teaching children to fold their hands and close their eyes helps them concentrate on prayer and stay out of trouble with siblings and friends.]

❑ When you pray, speak clearly, reverently, and pray in Jesus' name.
See Matthew 6:7-13 and 1 John 5:13-15.

❑ Speak of God and spiritual things in a respectful way. Use language which shows respect; use proper names; avoid profanity and minced oaths.
"Hear, for I will speak of excellent things; and the opening of my lips shall be right things" (Proverbs 8:6, KJV).

❑ Do not complain against the things God allows in your life: illness, plans interrupted, weather, circumstances, etc.

❑ Show respect for God's servants; treat them with special favor.
"Let the elders who rule well be considered worthy of double honor, especially those who work hard at preaching and teaching" (1 Timothy 5:17, NASB).

Attentiveness

"However you want people to treat you, so treat them, for this is the Law and the Prophets" (Matthew 7:12, NASB).

Ages 4-5

❑ Learn your name, address, and phone number; give this information only to the proper people.

❑ Do not ask strangers and family friends for things you want.

❑ Sit quietly at recitals, church services, story time, banquets, and programs — do not allow your personal "entertainment" to be a source of distraction to others in an audience.

Obedience

"Even a child is known by his doings, whether his work be pure, and whether it be right" (Proverbs 20:11, KJV).

Ages 4-5

❏ Use the words "May I" to ask permission.

❏ Answer with a simple "yes, sir" or "no, ma'am."

❏ Learn good table manners.

  ❏ Come to the table clean and neat.
  ❏ Unfold your napkin in half; place it on your lap.

- ❑ Do not begin to eat until after prayer and the hostess begins (exception: large group or expressed direction to do otherwise).
- ❑ Practice pleasant conversation at the table; choose appropriate topics.
- ❑ Avoid mashing foods together on your plate.
- ❑ Don't wash down food with your beverage.
- ❑ Don't use the serving utensils for personal use.
- ❑ Avoid eating only one type of food at a time.
- ❑ Chew with your mouth closed.
- ❑ Avoid talking with food in your mouth.

❑ Key to good table manners: How do I look to others while I am eating? Avoid any action that does not look pleasing when you observe others.

❑ Keep your room neat with clothes and toys properly put away.

❑ Clean up work and play areas immediately when projects are done.

*H*onesty

"Provide things honest in the sight of all men"
(Romans 12:17, KJV).

Ages 4-5

❑ Speak clearly, directly, and audibly. Leave baby talk behind. Do not whine when speaking. *". . . Except ye utter by the tongue words easy to be understood, how shall it be known what is spoken? . . ." (1 Corinthians 14:9, KJV).*

❑ Avoid using profanity and bad expressions.
"Thou shalt not take the name of the Lord thy God in vain . . ." (Exodus 20:7, KJV).
"Swear not at all . . . let your communication be, Yea, yea; Nay, nay: for whatsoever is more than these cometh of evil" (Matthew 5:34-37, KJV).

Loyalty

"Render therefore to all their dues: tribute to whom tribute is due; custom to whom custom; fear to whom fear; honour to whom honour" (Romans 13:7, KJV).

Ages 4-5

❏ Use words "excuse me" when you need to interrupt someone, when you have created a problem, or when you need to clear a path.

❏ Always knock on a closed door; wait for permission to enter.

❏ Address adults by title and surname; never call your parents by their first names.

❏ Always greet adults you know with a smile and answer their questions properly.

❑   Sit still in church.

"I write so that you may know how one ought to conduct himself in the household of God, which is the church of the living God" (1 Timothy 3:15, NASB).

❑   Unless your situation is an emergency, do not leave a service or special program to use the restroom. Visiting the restroom before a program will help avoid emergencies. If you do need to walk out, sit in the back when you return.

❑   Don't eat candy or chew gum during a church service or concert (exception: cough drops to keep you from disturbing people around you).

[Note to Parents: There is a distinct difference in relating to your children as a peer or "pal" and relating to them as an authority who loves them. You can never be a "buddy" to children and do the training job God intended. Be an "authority friend" to your child, not a "buddy friend."]

Gratefulness

"In every thing give thanks: for this is the will of God in Christ Jesus concerning you" (1 Thessalonians 5:18, KJV).

Ages 4-5

❑ Smiles are important; show a happy face to those around you no matter what the circumstances are.
"A joyful heart makes a cheerful face . . ." (Proverbs 15:13, NASB).
"A joyful heart is good medicine . . ." (Proverbs 17:22, NASB).

❑ Take a gift to a birthday party. Give the gift cheerfully.
". . . For God loves a cheerful giver" (2 Corinthians 9:7, NASB).

❑ Use items in the manner they were intended to be used.

$\mathcal{P}$atience

"And we urge you, brethren, admonish the unruly, encourage the fainthearted, help the weak, be patient with all men" (1 Thessalonians 5:14, NASB).

Ages 4-5

❏ Snack at snacktime; sleep at bedtime; play at playtime; eat at mealtime. Do the right thing at the right time. *(See Ecclesiastes 3:1-11.)*

❏ Respond kindly to the apologies of others.

❏ Never laugh at someone else's appearance, opinions, or mistakes.
". . . However you want people to treat you, so treat them . . ." (Matthew 7:12, NASB).

[Note to Parents: Be alert to discrepancies in demonstrating manners you are trying to train in your child. For example, a guest spills a cup; a child does—do you respond differently? Teach the art of pleasant conversation at the table. Do not interrupt your children's conversations. Treat your children as people.]

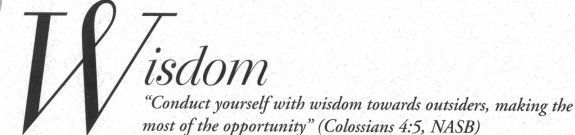

Wisdom

"Conduct yourself with wisdom towards outsiders, making the most of the opportunity" (Colossians 4:5, NASB)

Ages 6-8

❏ Keep secret the confidences of a friend.

"He who goes about as a talebearer reveals secrets, but he who is trustworthy conceals a matter" (Proverbs 11:13, NASB).
". . . A whisperer separateth chief friends" (Proverbs 16:28, KJV).

❏ Refuse to discuss private and personal matters.

"When there are many words, transgression is unavoidable" (Proverbs 10:19, NASB).
"For it is a shame even to speak of those things which are done of them in secret" (Ephesians 5:12, KJV).

❑ Refuse a "dare" with a Godly response.

"... do you not know that your body is a temple of the Holy Spirit who is in you, whom you have from God, and that you are not your own? For you have been bought with a price: therefore glorify God in your body" (1 Corinthians 6:19-20, NASB).

"My son, if sinners entice thee, consent thou not. ... walk not thou in the way with them; refrain thy foot from their path" (Proverbs 1:10-15, KJV).

$\mathcal{A}$ttentiveness

"However you want people to treat you, so treat them, for this is the Law and the Prophets" (Matthew 7:12, NASB).

Ages 6-8

❑ Answer the telephone clearly. Amplify cheerfulness, friendliness and respect with your voice because your face cannot be seen. (Hint: Smile as you talk; a smile will cause your voice to show a cheerful attitude.)

❑ Accurately record any messages, and be sure they are delivered.

❑ Do not eavesdrop. Do not repeat things you hear your parents or other adults say.
" But also gossips and busybodies, talking about things not proper to mention"
(1 Timothy 5:13, NASB).

❑ Follow through on all parental instructions.

❑ Avoid using a comb in public. Do repair jobs on your appearance in the restroom.

Obedience

"Even a child is known by his doings, whether his work be pure, and whether it be right" (Proverbs 20:11, KJV).

Ages 6-8

❏ Avoid "nope/yeah" type of casual responses to authority.

❏ When eating in a public place, eat quietly. Order within instructions about price limits. Place your order clearly and cheerfully.

❏ Learn good table manners.

    ❏ Sit up tall at the table; avoid hunching over your plate as if guarding it.

    ❏ Keep elbows off the table until the meal is ended.

    ❏ Serve yourself small portions at first; have seconds later.

- ❏ Cut your own food, 2-3 bites at a time; change utensils to proper hand to eat (American zigzag method).

  [Note to parents: European eating style varies from American. In Europe, a person uses his knife in the right hand and his fork in the left. Americans "zigzag" the use of hands by cutting with the right hand and then laying the knife down to pick up the fork. As you deem necessary, these distinctions can be practiced with your children.]

- ❏ Transfer butter to your plate, then to your bread or food.
- ❏ Pass food to the right or by way of the shortest distance to the person who made the request.
- ❏ Avoid reaching in front of another person's plate to get a serving dish.
- ❏ Don't help yourself first (without asking permission) when passing a requested dish.
- ❏ Tip soup or cereal bowl away from you; dip spoon away from you; avoid slurping.

- ❏ You may drink soup from a bowl if it has handles like a cup and there are no chunks in the liquid.
- ❏ Never dunk your food unless you are eating alone or food was designed for it.
- ❏ If at the table, eat french fries with a fork and use a spoon to eat berries. Remove pits from your mouth with your fingers.
- ❏ Butter only one section of a corn cob at a time; pick it up with fingers to eat.
- ❏ Eat chicken with fingers only if the hostess does, and if it is fried—crispy.
- ❏ Avoid cutting spaghetti; twist it onto your fork one biteful at a time.
- ❏ Break bread before buttering and eating (exception: a hot roll may be buttered in its entirety while hot, then broken and eaten).
- ❏ Remove a foreign object or unchewable object from your mouth with your fingers; place it at the side of your plate.
- ❏ Place used silverware in the center of your plate.

❏   When you have finished eating, do not push your plate away.

❏   Place your napkin neatly by the side of your plate after the meal. Do not refold it.

❏   Say "thank you" to the hostess for the meal; ask to be excused from the table.

❏   In a buffet line, take only one serving at a time. Wait until everyone has been served before going for seconds.

❏   Keep clean—bathe yourself, wash your hair, and brush your teeth regularly. *"For God hath not called us to uncleanness, but unto holiness" (1 Thessalonians 4:7, KJV).*

❏   Clean up immediately after all projects (for example, cooking, art projects, science experiments, etc.).

❏   Be careful not to leave a mess behind you in church: pick up your programs, return songbooks to the rack, etc.

$\mathcal{H}$onesty

"Provide things honest in the sight of all men"
(Romans 12:17, KJV).

Ages 6-8

❑ Avoid using slang expressions. Learn which words are right to use in specific circumstances.

❑ Avoid using nicknames which focus on embarrassing characteristics of friends.

❑ Avoid teasing where both "giver and receiver" cannot enjoy the fun.
"A brother offended is harder to be won than a strong city . . ." (Proverbs 18:19, KJV).
"It is as sport for a fool to do mischief; but a man of understanding hath wisdom"
(Proverbs 10:23, KJV).

Loyalty

"Render therefore to all their dues: tribute to whom tribute is due; custom to whom custom; fear to whom fear; honour to whom honour" *(Romans 13:7, KJV).*

Ages 6-8

❏ Ask permission of the hostess (your mother) before inviting friends to the house.

❏ Ask permission before volunteering others.

❏ Dress up for church to show respect to the Lord; dress up for special occasions to show respect for the person being honored.

❏ Participate in all aspects of the church service with enthusiasm: singing, listening, giving, worship, responding.
"I was glad when they said unto me, Let us go into the house of the Lord" (Psalm 122:1, KJV).
"Enter into his gates with thanksgiving, and into his courts with praise . . ."
(Psalm 100:4-5, KJV).

❏ Come into the service quietly.

❏ Sit for a moment of silent prayer.

❏ Listen quietly to the prelude and offertory.

❏ Smile a welcome to friends; visit when the service is ended.

❏ When visiting other churches, you are not required to follow their rituals.

❏ If you are late, wait for the proper time to be seated. Do not walk into the auditorium during prayer, a solo, a choir anthem, or the sermon. If you know that you will need to leave the service early, sit in the back row.

Gratefulness

"In every thing give thanks: for this is the will of God in Christ Jesus concerning you" (1 Thessalonians 5:18, KJV).

Ages 6-8

❑ Write thank you notes to acknowledge gifts, favors, and kindnesses of others: overnight hospitality—within 2-3 days; birthday—within 1 week; Christmas—within 2 weeks.

❑ Accept a compliment with a smile and a sincere "thank you." Do not insult the giver with a negative response.

❑ Dinner is a time for family conversation; do not bring up problems or watch television. Give yourself attentively to your family. Appropriate background music is desirable.

❑ Show cheerfulness to family guests.

Patience

"And we urge you, brethren, admonish the unruly, encourage the fainthearted, help the weak, be patient with all men" (1 Thessalonians 5:14, NASB).

Ages 6-8

❏ Never call attention to someone else's blunder.

❏ Apologize briefly and sincerely for an accident. (Profuse apology only irritates; accidents happen to everyone.)

❏ Let older people precede you through a door.

❏ Let older people serve themselves first in a buffet line. Go through a buffet line with your parents.

Wisdom

"Conduct yourself with wisdom towards outsiders, making the most of the opportunity" (Colossians 4:5, NASB)

Ages 9-11

❏ Distinguish between humor and folly. Avoid practical jokes.
"Answer not a fool according to his folly, lest thou also be like unto him"
(Proverbs 26:4, KJV).
"The thought of foolishness is sin . . ." (Proverbs 24:9, KJV).

❏ Distinguish levels of casualness in dress.
". . . Man looketh on the outward appearance, but the Lord looketh on the heart"
(1 Samuel 16:7, KJV).

❑ Understand how your dress influences your conduct and others' perception of you.

❑ Differentiate sub-casual, casual, business and church attire. Know when and where each type of outfit is appropriate; strive to fit in (with discretion) the community in which you live.

❑ Avoid fads in dress and hairstyle.

*A*ttentiveness

"However you want people to treat you, so treat them, for this is the Law and the Prophets" (Matthew 7:12, NASB).

Ages 9-11

❑ Learn to introduce people to one another. Use the "name-first" technique: Say first the name of the person you need to honor most in the situation. Present the other person to that person.

     ❑ Friend to parent—say parent's name first.

     ❑ Friend to friend—say girl's name first or say older friend's name first.

     ❑ Friend to Pastor—say Pastor's name first.

     ❑ Friend to adult—say adult's name first.

❏ Give a conversational start to the people you've just introduced.

❏ Shake hands firmly with eye contact, briefly and sincerely: always when a man greets a man and always when a woman extends her hand first.

❏ Remove your hat: when you enter a building, when you greet a lady, when you are introduced for the first time, when the flag goes by or the national anthem is played, any time you need to show respect.

❏ A gentleman should offer his seat to a lady: who is standing in travel, who is traveling with small children, who is standing where seats have not been purchased.

❏   Offer your seat to anyone who is elderly or handicapped.

❏   Know when to end a visit.
"Withdraw thy foot from thy neighbor's house; lest he be weary of thee, and so hate thee"
(Proverbs 25:17, KJV).

      ❏   Drop-in: 1 hour limit.
      ❏   Dinner: 2 hour limit or 1 hour after dinner has ended.
      ❏   Overnight visit: do not extend the agreed time.

❏   Volunteer to be helpful: open the door for a lady; open the door for a person carrying heavy packages; assist with small children; assist the elderly or handicapped; meet the needs of others as you perceive them.

❏   Keep the volume of games and music to considerate levels.

Obedience

"Even a child is known by his doings, whether his work be pure, and whether it be right" (Proverbs 20:11, KJV).

Ages 9-11

❏ Observe lights out and rising times.
"My son, observe the commandment of your father, and do not forsake the teaching of your mother ...." (Proverbs 6:20-23, NASB).

❏ Maintain personal cleanliness—regular bath, shampoo, clean clothes and orderly room.

❏ Be on time for meals and appointments.

❏ Do not visit with friends when a person is speaking or performing.

❑ Prepare for elegant eating situations by practicing good table manners:

     ❑ Seat the lady at your right before seating yourself (gentlemen).

     ❑ Silverware is arranged from "outside in" in order of need to use it. Watch the hostess for special clues.

     ❑ Between courses, leave silverware from previous course in center of plate or on edge of the liner plate to indicate that you have finished. Keep your butter knife on the bread plate.

     ❑ At a family-style meal, be alert to pass food before being asked.

     ❑ Use the finger bowl for fingers only, one hand at a time. Dry your fingers on your napkin.

     ❑ Specialty food items: watch hostess for clues. Eat shrimp with a fork.

- ❑ Do not eat ice cubes or suck crushed ice.
- ❑ Use bread/butter plate for rolls, and place finger relishes there.
- ❑ You may cut salad with a knife. Then change utensils "zigzag style" to eat your salad.
- ❑ Once a utensil has been used, never return it to the tablecloth.
- ❑ Avoid building silverware "planks" from the table to your plate.
- ❑ If you drop a utensil, simply apologize and ask the hostess or server for another.
- ❑ Do not discuss dieting or special diets at the table. Avoid topics which would cause any other dinner guest to become ill or offended.
- ❑ Saying grace publicly should be done reverently without ostentatiousness, and sincerely.

Honesty

"Provide things honest in the sight of all men"
(Romans 12:17, KJV).

Ages 9-11

❑ Avoid double-meaning jokes.
"The lips of the righteous bring forth what is acceptable, but the mouth of the wicked, what is perverted" *(Proverbs 10:32, NASB).*

"A naughty person, a wicked man, walketh with a froward mouth. . . . Therefore shall his calamity come suddenly . . ." *(Proverbs 6:12-15, KJV).*

❏ Practice good conversation habits.

"But I say unto you, That every idle word that men shall speak, they shall give account thereof in the day of judgment. For by thy words thou shalt be justified, and by thy words thou shalt be condemned" (Matthew 12:36-37, KJV).

"Let your speech be always with grace, seasoned with salt, that ye may know how ye ought to answer every man" (Colossians 4:6. KJV).

❏ Contribute to the conversation in progress. Avoid changing the subject without asking permission of the participants.

❏ Always use standard English vocabulary and grammar. Mentally correct errors you hear so they won't lodge in your subconscious memory.

    ❏ Use colloquialisms only in very informal situations.

    ❏ Never use slang, profanity, or vulgar expressions.

    ❏ Never use poor grammar—even for effect.

❏ Use correct voice placement, volume, and appropriate speed of speech.

❏ Use words the hearers will understand.

❏ In controversial situations, rephrase what you have heard before answering to ensure correct understanding.

"He who gives an answer before he hears, it is folly and shame to him" (Proverbs 18:13, NASB).

❏ *RSVP*—requires written or telephone response indicating whether or not you will accept. *Regrets only*—requires written or telephone response only if you cannot accept the invitation.

*L*oyalty

"Render therefore to all their dues: tribute to whom tribute is due; custom to whom custom; fear to whom fear; honour to whom honour" (Romans 13:7, KJV).

Ages 9-11

❏ Greet adults before they greet you.

❏ Stand—when a person of authority enters a room, when introduced to an adult, or when a lady enters the room (gentlemen).

❏ Avoid the use of slang terms to refer to people in authority (for example, "cop, the teach, my old man, the fuzz," etc.) *See Romans 13:1-7.*

❏ Respect the privacy of others—mail, permission to use personal items, etc.

Gratefulness

"In every thing give thanks: for this is the will of God in Christ Jesus concerning you" (1 Thessalonians 5:18, KJV).

Ages 9-11

❏ Give sincerely to honor others. Do not give with the hope of return or the desire to impress. *"The generous man will be prosperous, and he who holds water will himself be watered" (Proverbs 11:25, NASB).*

❏ Give gifts that cost you something, but give what you can afford. Your giving should express a heart of love and gratefulness.
". . . Nay, but I will surely buy it of thee at a price: neither will I offer . . . that which doth cost me nothing" (2 Samuel 24:24, KJV).
"Owe nothing to anyone except to love one another . . ." (Romans 13:8, NASB).

❏ In receiving gifts, value the giver more than the gift. Always express gratefulness.

❏ Practice good hospitality habits.
"Use hospitality one to another without grudging" (1 Peter 4:9, KJV).

❏ Offer to help guests, but do not pressure them if your offer is refused.

❏ Respect the time and property of the guest; respect the privacy of the guest.

❏ Develop points of interest for conversing with the guest.

❏ Plan appropriate activities to enjoy with your guest.

❏ Wherever possible, be flexible in allowing your guest to make choices. Be gracious when you must refuse an option.

❏ Offer to serve refreshments for visitors who have come to see your parents.

❏ When someone in your household has a visitor, do not stay after greeting the person unless you are invited to do so.

❏ Practice excellent personal correspondence habits:
"Rejoice with them that do rejoice; weep with them that weep" (Romans 12:15, KJV).

❏ Use proper supplies.

❏ Handwritten work must be legible.

❏ Answer promptly.

❏ Learn to express joy, sympathy, personal feelings without wordiness. Refer to a standard manual for proper forms.

❏ Refer to a current etiquette manual for accurate forms of salutation, address, and abbreviations (e.g. Mrs. George Bush, not Mrs. Barbara Bush).

❏ Do not send cards with just a name signed across the bottom. Always include a short personal note.

Patience

"And we urge you, brethren, admonish the unruly, encourage the fainthearted, help the weak, be patient with all men" (1 Thessalonians 5:14, NASB).

Ages 9-11

❏ Be gracious in response to reproof or correction—whether or not you feel it was deserved.
"Whoever loves discipline loves knowledge, but he who hates reproof is stupid"
(Proverbs 12:1, NASB).

"A fool rejects his father's discipline, but he who regards reproof is prudent" (Proverbs 15:5, NASB)

"He whose ear listens to the life-giving reproof will dwell among the wise. He who neglects discipline despises himself, but he who listens to reproof acquires understanding"
(Proverbs 15:31-32, NASB).

❏ When you do not wish to answer a personal question inappropriately asked, simply say, "I'd rather not say" in a calm, pleasant voice. Do not feel obligated to answer such questions.

❏ Avoid arguments.
"... *The forcing of wrath bringeth forth strife*" (Proverbs 30:33, KJV).
"*A gentle answer turns away wrath, but a harsh word stirs up anger*" (Proverbs 15:1, NASB).
"*A fool's lips enter into contention, and his mouth calleth for strokes*" (Proverbs 18:6, KJV).

  ❏ Think twice before speaking. Keep the real issue in view.
  "*But refuse foolish and ignorant speculations, knowing that they produce quarrels*" (2 Timothy 2:23, NASB).

  ❏ Never allow yourself to become offensively dogmatic.
  "*If possible, so far as it depends on you, be at peace with all men*" (Romans 12:18, NASB).

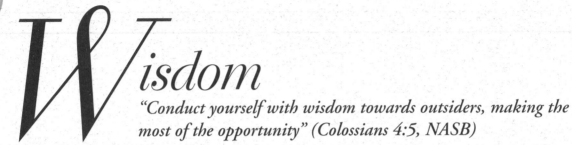

Wisdom

"Conduct yourself with wisdom towards outsiders, making the most of the opportunity" (Colossians 4:5, NASB)

Ages 11 - 14

❏ Make only those commitments of which God and your parents would approve.

❏ Say "no" firmly, but kindly, to those things which you cannot do.

❏ Do not make commitments which you know you have little chance of being able to fulfill.
"Do not be hasty in word or impulsive in thought . . . let your words be few . . . Pay what you vow" (Ecclesiastes 5:1-2, 4-6, NASB).
"Lord, Who shall abide in thy tabernacle? Who shall dwell in thy holy hill? . . . he that sweareth to his own hurt and changeth not" (Psalm 14:1, 4, KJV).

❏ Learn to be a good friend. Do not violate appropriate degrees of friendship: authority, buddy, acquaintance, close friends, etc. Avoid undue familiarity.

"Honour thy father and mother" (Ephesians 6:2, KJV)
"Servants, be obedient to them that are your masters" (Ephesians 6:5, KJV).
"A friend loveth at all times" (Proverbs 17:17, KJV).
"Faithful are the wounds of a friend" (Proverbs 27:6, KJV).
"Do not forsake your own friend or your father's friend" (Proverbs 27:10, NASB).
"Iron sharpens iron, so one man sharpens another" (Proverbs 27:17, NASB).

❏ To refuse a drink or cigarette, simply say, "No, thank you." If asked why, then simply state your conviction. It is never necessary to apologize for refusing. Refuse the "gift"—not the giver!

"A gentle answer turns away wrath" (Proverbs 15:1, NASB).
"Your body is the temple of the Holy Spirit . . . ye are not your own" (1 Corinthians 6:19-20. KJV).

❏ Strive for a natural look in the use of cosmetics, realizing that simplicity and good taste will enhance a Godly countenance.

"And not let your adornment be merely external—braiding the hair, and wearing gold jewelry, or putting on dresses; but let it be the hidden person of the heart, with the imperishable quality of a gentle and quiet spirit, which is precious in the sight of God" (1 Peter 3:3-4, NASB).

Attentiveness

"However you want people to treat you, so treat them, for this is the Law and the Prophets" (Matthew 7:12, NASB).

Ages 11-14

❑ Observe wise procedures in participating in social events:

    ❑ Plan carefully all activities of the occasion.

    ❑ Invite people directly, stating plans clearly.

    ❑ If you must refuse an invitation, do so kindly and clearly. It is not necessary to explain, but be as helpful as is possible to be.

    ❑ Be punctual both to call and be called for.

    ❑ Never cancel one appointment to accept another.

    ❑ Observe curfew times.

❏ Know the rules for introducing people with special titles; "name first" principle will still apply (see rules for introductions in *attentiveness* section, ages 9-11).

❏ If you forget a name, simply apologize graciously and ask to be reminded.

❏ Do not play guessing games with people to whom you are introducing yourself.

❏ If you have been erroneously introduced, graciously correct the information.

❏ If you forget the order of introduction, simply adjust the sentence to accommodate: "Mr. Young, I'd like to have you meet Mr. Elder."

❏ Never apply cosmetics or use a comb in public.

Obedience

"Even a child is known by his doings, whether his work be pure, and whether it be right" (Proverbs 20:11, KJV).

Ages 11-14

❑ A man should precede a woman in situations involving potential danger: stepping off bus/train/airplane (with outside steps), stepping off crowded elevator, leading into dark areas, leading up and down staircases.

❑ When walking with a woman, a man walks on the curbside of the street.

❑ Avoid walking on the grass in public places.

❑ Do not litter in public places; always be conscious of picking up after yourself.

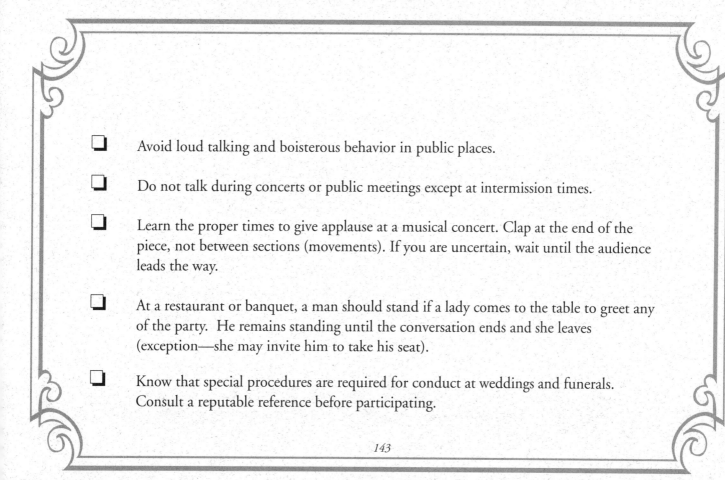

❏   Avoid loud talking and boisterous behavior in public places.

❏   Do not talk during concerts or public meetings except at intermission times.

❏   Learn the proper times to give applause at a musical concert. Clap at the end of the piece, not between sections (movements). If you are uncertain, wait until the audience leads the way.

❏   At a restaurant or banquet, a man should stand if a lady comes to the table to greet any of the party. He remains standing until the conversation ends and she leaves (exception—she may invite him to take his seat).

❏   Know that special procedures are required for conduct at weddings and funerals. Consult a reputable reference before participating.

*H*onesty

"Provide things honest in the sight of all men"
(Romans 12:17, KJV).

Ages 11-14

❑   Be conscientious about payment of calls you make from another's telephone.

❑   Dress modestly so that it is easy for others to keep their attention on your face.

❑   Know how to handle controversial topics of conversation:

         ❑   Do not argue or be offensively dogmatic.
         ❑   Reject firmly and kindly any topic of conversation which violates modesty or propriety.

❏ Reject any topic of conversation about which your spirit does not feel at ease. Say, "I'd rather not discuss that."

❏ Reject any topic of conversation which violates God's commandments—gossip, slander, evil report, critical spirit, etc.

❏ If the response to a kind, but firm rejection of a topic is not good, excuse yourself politely and walk away.

❏ Avoid flirtatiousness (winking, teasing, inappropriate body language).
"A worthless person, a wicked man, is the one who walks with a false mouth, who winks with his eyes, who signals with his feet, who points with his fingers . . ." (Proverbs 6:12-13, NASB).

"Put away from you a deceitful mouth . . . let your eyes look directly ahead . . . watch the path of your feet" (Proverbs 4:24-26, NASB).

❏ Express naturally a sincere interest in others.

*L*oyalty

"Render therefore to all their dues: tribute to whom tribute is due; custom to whom custom; fear to whom fear; honour to whom honour" (Romans 13:7, KJV).

Ages 11-14

❑ When family standards and a friend's standards conflict, explain your convictions quietly without a condescending spirit.

❑ Live your convictions consistently without a judgmental spirit.
"Do not judge lest you be judged. For in the way you judge, you will be judged; and by your standard of measure, it will be measured to you" (Matthew 7:1-2, NASB).

❑ Commit yourself to the ways of God.

"Let no one look down on your youthfulness, but rather in speech, conduct, love, faith and purity, show yourself an example of those who believe" (1 Timothy 4:12, NASB).

❑ Give witness to the truth of salvation in your life with warmth and sincerity, showing compassion without a spirit of condescension.
"But sanctify the Lord God in your hearts: and be ready always to give an answer to every man that asketh you a reason of the hope that is in you with meekness and fear" (1 Peter 3:15, KJV).

❑ Do not "argue religion." Allow the Holy Spirit to develop the content of your testimony and bring conviction to the listener on His timetable.

❑ Be conscious of the effect of your actions on the receipt of your words.
"Let not then your good be evil spoken of" (Romans 14:16, KJV).
"The fruit of the righteous is a tree of life; and he that winneth souls is wise" (Proverbs 11:30, KJV).
See also the "Great Commission," Matthew 28:18-20.

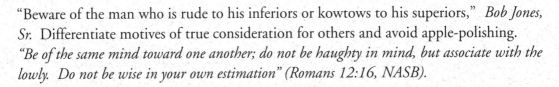

❏ "Beware of the man who is rude to his inferiors or kowtows to his superiors," *Bob Jones, Sr.* Differentiate motives of true consideration for others and avoid apple-polishing. *"Be of the same mind toward one another; do not be haughty in mind, but associate with the lowly. Do not be wise in your own estimation" (Romans 12:16, NASB).*

". . . Not to think of himself more highly than he ought to think . . . we, being many, are one body in Christ, and every one members one of another" (Romans 12:3-5, KJV).

"Do not hold your faith . . . with attitude of personal favoritism" (James 2:1, NASB).

Gratefulness

"In every thing give thanks: for this is the will of God in Christ Jesus concerning you" (1 Thessalonians 5:18, KJV).

Ages 11-14

❏ Recognize that tipping is an expression of gratefulness for services rendered. It is not a substitute for words of gratefulness to be expressed. If a tip is ever withheld, a kind and constructive explanation should be given.

❏ Behave wisely in public places so that you may leave a tract without fear of detracting from the Gospel of Jesus Christ. *(See 1 Peter 3:12-17.)*

❏ Do not give flattery; give sincere words of praise.
"Meddle not with him that flattereth with his lips" (Proverbs 20:19, KJV).
"A flattering mouth worketh ruin" (Proverbs 26:28, KJV).

❏ Be a considerate guest in the home of others:

      ❏ Follow the family schedule.

      ❏ Pay your own way: telephone, special entertainment, special foods or medications you may require, etc.

      ❏ Offer to help, but do not force your assistance.

      ❏ Make your own bed; keep your area neat; pick up after yourself.

      ❏ If offered a choice, make one graciously and clearly.

      ❏ Respect the privacy of the family and family property. Do not borrow items without permission.

$\mathcal{P}$atience

"And we urge you, brethren, admonish the unruly, encourage the fainthearted, help the weak, be patient with all men" (1 Thessalonians 5:14, NASB).

Ages 11-14

❏ Do not correct or rebuke an older person.
"Rebuke not an elder . . ." (1 Timothy 5:1, KJV).

❏ Correct a child only when you have been given the right to do so and only in the prescribed manner of the authority delegated.

❏ Correct another person in a spirit of humility.
". . . restore such a one in a spirit of gentleness; each one looking to yourself, lest you too be tempted" (Galatians 6:1, NASB).

❑ Make corrections with constructive suggestions and Godly instruction (in the spirit of Ephesians 6:4 and 9).

❑ Make corrections without anger.
"For the wrath of men worketh not the righteousness of God" (James 1:20, KJV).

❑ Plan your schedule carefully, pacing activities to minimize impatient responses.

❑ Give your expectations to God.
"The Lord will perfect that which concerneth me: thy mercy, O Lord endureth for ever: forsake not the works of thine own hands" (Psalm 138:8, KJV).

"Being confident of this very thing, that He which hath begun a good work in you will perform it until the day of Jesus Christ" (Philippians 1:6, KJV).

"He hath shown thee, O man, what is good; and what doth the Lord require of thee, but to do justly, and to love mercy, and to walk humbly with thy God?" (Micah 6:8, KJV).

❑ Avoid writing the following types of letters: angry, accusatory, confessional. Deal with these items in gracious personal confrontation.

Wisdom

"Conduct yourself with wisdom towards outsiders, making the most of the opportunity" (Colossians 4:5, NASB)

Ages 14-18

❑ Balance friendliness and caution in dealing with strangers.

❑ Consult a reputable reference for forms and procedures needed in persuasive letter writing (e.g. editorials, appeals, complaints).

❑ Involve family members in your friendships with the opposite gender.

❑ Focus discussions with friends on ideas, books, principles, ministry projects, etc. Do not discuss people or intimate personal topics.

Attentiveness

"However you want people to treat you, so treat them, for this is the Law and the Prophets" (Matthew 7:12, NASB).

Ages 14-18

❏ Observe wise procedures in courtship activities:

    ❏ A man should obtain permission from the lady's father before approaching her with any invitation. Deal directly with the lady's father about all details of permission and arrangements.

    ❏ If you are attending a formal event, ask the color of her dress before ordering flowers.

    ❏ Call for a lady at the door and visit with her family.

❏   Avoid plans which isolate you as a young couple. Plan for proper chaperonage.
"Giving no offence in any thing, that the ministry be not blamed"
(2 Corinthians 6:3, KJV).

"Flee also youthful lusts" (2 Timothy 2:22, KJV).

❏   Avoid long periods of discussion; plan wholesome activities instead.

❏   Apply all the rules which accompany courteous participation in any social event.

❏   Address a person you meet with the correct name and title until you are invited to use casual or nickname reference.

❏   Avoid trite responses when you have been introduced to new people.

❏   Avoid name-dropping.
See James 2:1-3.

Obedience

"Even a child is known by his doings, whether his work be pure, and whether it be right" (Proverbs 20:11, KJV).

Ages 14-18

❑ Learn good business etiquette—manners for the job: *(See Ephesians 6:5-9.)*

    ❑ Dress according to expressed requirements.

    ❑ Keep relationships professional.

    ❑ Employee and employer—each should present the other in the best possible light.

    ❑ Observe time limits. Give a full day's work for a full day's wage.

    ❑ Observe levels of authority. Don't be presumptuous in the use of first names or practice of special privileges.

❏   Keep your personal life outside the work place.

❏   Correct problems privately.

❏   Observe proper telephone courtesy. Consult a reputable reference manual.

❏ Women in business should graciously balance femininity and efficiency.
See Titus 2:3-5.

❏ Learn excellent application and interview procedures. Consult a reputable reference manual.

❏ Practice good restaurant etiquette:

     ❏   In mixed company, a man leads the way to a table if no host/hostess is available.

     ❏   A man should seat a lady in the choice seat.

     ❏   A man should place the lady's order, although she should answer direct questions about choice of salad dressing, preparation of meat, style of vegetable, etc.

- ☐ A lady never places her purse or gloves on the table.
- ☐ A lady should ask subtly for price clues when ordering: "What do you recommend?" or "What sounds good?" Then order within the price range of the answer.
- ☐ "Table d'hote" means all courses, beverages, etc. included in meal price.
- ☐ "Ala carte" means each course of menu and beverage are priced separately.
- ☐ Men should check their coats if possible; women may keep theirs if they wish.
- ☐ When a woman desires to pay for a meal, she should plan ahead re: best procedure for avoiding embarrassment to the man or the server.
- ☐ If a restaurant menu is too expensive for you, explain quietly to the waiter that you will not be dining there and leave. Do not walk out without an explanation.

Honesty

"Provide things honest in the sight of all men"
(Romans 12:17, KJV).

Ages 14-18

❏ Differentiate gifts, bribes, and rewards. Learn to give an appropriate, gracious response in each situation.

❏ Always notify the party if you are unable to keep an appointment or obligation. Call if you will be late for a meeting. Make a personal contact if payment or other obligation is overdue.

❏ Learn parliamentary procedure—proper protocol for public meetings and controlled discussion. Consult *Robert's Rules of Order* as a reference.

Loyalty

"Render therefore to all their dues: tribute to whom tribute is due; custom to whom custom; fear to whom fear; honour to whom honour" *(Romans 13:7, KJV).*

Ages 14-18

❏ Avoid discussing personal issues in public.

❏ Avoid criticizing family members in public.

❏ Don't discuss personal problems with people who are neither part of the problem nor part of the solution.

Gratefulness

"In every thing give thanks: for this is the will of God in Christ Jesus concerning you" (1 Thessalonians 5:18, KJV).

Ages 14-18

❏ Hostess gifts are small tokens of thoughtfulness given when attending a dinner or staying overnight. These are optional, but recommended.

❏ When giving gifts in a "courting" relationship, purchase inexpensive and impersonal items. Give without obligation of return; give to communicate friendliness. Never accept expensive gifts which violate the degree of friendship which has been developed. Kindly, but firmly return such a gift with the statement, "I cannot keep this." If necessary, you can add, "My parents would not allow it."

❑ Entertain as a ministry to others.
"Do not neglect to show hospitality to strangers, for by this some have entertained angels without knowing it" (Hebrews 13:2, NASB).

"But when you give a reception, invite the poor, the crippled, the lame, the blind, and you will be blessed, since they do not have the means to repay you; for you will be repaid at the resurrection of the righteous" (Luke 14:13-14, NASB).

❑ Do what you are able to do in entertaining.

❑ Do not compare levels of entertainment with others; do not compete.

❏   In serving food when entertaining:

      ❏   Use the most convenient way possible.

      ❏   Serve carefully and cheerfully.

      ❏   Remove all serving dishes before offering the dessert.

      ❏   Avoid scraping dishes at the table.

      ❏   Do not wash dishes while guests are still present.

*P*atience

"And we urge you, brethren, admonish the unruly, encourage the fainthearted, help the weak, be patient with all men" (1 Thessalonians 5:14, NASB).

Ages 14-18

❑ Be courteous when driving:

  ❑ Yield right of way; wait your turn.

  ❑ Signal your intentions properly.

  ❑ Allow enough time for travel.

  ❑ Allow for pedestrians and bicyclists.

  ❑ Dim lights for oncoming traffic.

❏ Do not become too absorbed in conversation within vehicle.

❏ Observe all rules of the road. Consult the motor vehicle division in your state for a booklet describing specific procedures.

❏ Throw nothing from the windows.

❏ Passengers should be considerate of the needs of the driver.

❏ Practice good etiquette in commuting:

❏ Be conscious of the rights and needs of others.

❏ In a taxi it is not necessary to make conversation with the driver.

Wisdom

"Conduct yourself with wisdom towards outsiders, making the most of the opportunity" (Colossians 4:5, NASB)

Ages 18 - Adulthood

❏ Avoid discussing marriage until parental approval has been given.

❏ When living alone, do not invite a person of the opposite gender into your home when no one else is present. Be conscious of other potentially compromising situations from the standpoint of impression created and personal vulnerability.

*A*ttentiveness

"However you want people to treat you, so treat them, for this is the Law and the Prophets" (Matthew 7:12, NASB).

Ages 18 - Adulthood

❑ In most circumstances, a man should ask a lady's father for permission prior to giving her a marriage proposal.

❑ Public displays of affection should be carefully limited to that which would not embarrass others. [Note: Most physical displays of affection should be reserved for marriage if young people want to honor Biblical standards of purity. However, it is possible that even hand-holding, sitting in close proximity at events, or gazing into one another's eyes could be awkward for observers. Engaged and married couples should be considerate of good taste.]

❑   Be a good tourist when traveling abroad:

    ❑   Don't expect people to speak English.

    ❑   Don't be ostentatious in dress.

    ❑   Don't assume you may wear anything you desire.

    ❑   Don't expect things to be like they are at home; avoid unfavorable comparisons.

    [Note: In cross-cultural situations, you may find that etiquette procedures will be vastly different from home. Adapt yourself to the situation as much as possible.]

    ❑   Don't expect to buy something for nothing.

    ❑   Don't take pictures of local people or their homes without permission.

    ❑   Be an ambassador of good will!

    "Now then we are ambassadors for Christ, as though God did beseech you by us; we pray you in Christ's stead, be ye reconciled to God" (2 Corinthians 5:20, KJV).

Obedience

"Even a child is known by his doings, whether his work be pure, and whether it be right" (Proverbs 20:11, KJV).

Ages 18 - Adulthood

❑ Prepare a concise, readable resume of your work experience:

    ❑ Use a word processor and laser printer if at all possible.

    ❑ Use quality paper in a businesslike color.

    ❑ Plan a "clean" layout with eye appeal.

    ❑ Proofread carefully.

    ❑ Accompany with a specific cover letter.

❏ Hand deliver if possible. If not, mail flat (unfolded).

❏ Follow up with a telephone call within 8 to 10 working days.

Resource: *Apprenticeship PLUS+* training course (available from *Education PLUS+*).

❏ Observe ethical practices in your job search and subsequent employment. Consult the employee handbook where you are hired.

Additional resource: *Career Pathways* program (available from *Christian Financial Concepts*).

Honesty

"Provide things honest in the sight of all men"
(Romans 12:17, KJV).

Ages 18 - Adulthood

❑ Practice all the cautions of good etiquette and responsibility when organizing life with roommates. Address questions before situations become problematic.

  ❑ Share the workload in maintaining living quarters. Clean up after yourself.
  ❑ Equitably divide costs of rent, utilities, food, supplies, etc. Live within your means.

❑ Be considerate when the other is entertaining friends. If you are not invited, make yourself constructively scarce.

❑ Be considerate of noise levels (television, radio, stereo system, etc.).

❑ Discuss and be willing to be flexible about adjusting irritating habits.

❑ Communicate openly and clearly about schedules, obligations, expenses, expectations , etc. Put agreements into written form to minimize misunderstandings.

Loyalty

"Render therefore to all their dues: tribute to whom tribute is due; custom to whom custom; fear to whom fear; honour to whom honour" *(Romans 13:7, KJV)*.

Ages 18 - Adulthood

❑ In marriage and family relationships, treat each person with the same level of respect/courtesy you would give to someone you really desire to impress. Give your best to your own.

"But if anyone does not provide for his own, and especially for those of his household, he has denied the faith and is worse than an unbeliever" (1 Timothy 5:8, NASB).

*G*ratefulness

"In every thing give thanks: for this is the will of God in Christ Jesus concerning you" (1 Thessalonians 5:18, KJV).

Ages 18 - Adulthood

❑   Demonstrate the courtesies of chivalry and ladylikeness throughout married life.

❑   Express genuine praise to your spouse and children. Avoid flattery.

Patience

"And we urge you, brethren, admonish the unruly, encourage the fainthearted, help the weak, be patient with all men" (1 Thessalonians 5:14, NASB).

Ages 18 - Adulthood

❑ Discipline children privately or as unobtrusively as possible. Avoid public reprimand whenever possible.

❑ Respond as graciously as possible to the needs of others, in terms of time extensions, broken promises, and flexibility of procedures. Learn how to develop "contingency plans."

❑ Be alert to opportunities for discipleship and mentoring. Invest time and attention in the lives of others.

Certificate of Achievement

In recognition of diligent effort to apply consistently the Etiquette PLUS rules outlined from Conception to Age 3, we the parents of

_____

award this Certificate of Achievement on the _____ day of the month of _____ in the Year _____

_____   _____

Certificate of Achievement

In recognition of diligent effort to apply consistently the Etiquette PLUS
rules outlined for Ages 4–5, we the parents of

_____

award this Certificate of Achievement on the _____ day
of the month of _____ in the Year _____

_____   _____

Certificate of Achievement

In recognition of diligent effort to apply consistently the Etiquette PLUS rules outlined for Ages 6–8, we the parents of

_____

award this Certificate of Achievement on the _____ day of the month of _____ in the Year _____

_____   _____

Certificate of Achievement

In recognition of diligent effort to apply consistently the Etiquette PLUS rules outlined for Ages 9–11, we the parents of

_____

award this Certificate of Achievement on the _____ day of the month of _____ in the Year _____

_____   _____

Certificate of Achievement

In recognition of diligent effort to apply consistently the Etiquette PLUS
rules outlined for Ages 11–14, we the parents of

_____

award this Certificate of Achievement on the _____ day
of the month of _____ in the Year _____

_____   _____

Certificate of Achievement

In recognition of diligent effort to apply consistently the Etiquette PLUS rules outlined for Ages 14–18, we the parents of

_____

award this Certificate of Achievement on the _____ day of the month of _____ in the Year _____

_____   _____